It's Up To You:

Developing Assertive Social Skills

Eileen D. Gambrill

Cheryl A. Richey

LES FEMMES
Millbrae, California

Published by Les Femmes Publishing
231 Adrian Road
Millbrae, California 94030

First Printing, September 1976
Made in the United States of America

Library of Congress Cataloging in Publication Data

Gambrill, Eileen D   1934–
    It's up to you.

    Bibliography: p.
    1. Interpersonal communication.   2. Assertiveness
(Psychology) I. Richey, Cheryl A., joint author.
II. Title.
BF637.C45G35   158'.2   75-37069
ISBN 0-89087-913-3

1 2 3 4 5 6 7 8 — 82 81 80 79 78 77 76

Contents

Preface

We decided to write this handbook because we were impressed by the remarkable number of people we heard from who were dissatisfied with their social contacts. They raised very basic questions such as *how* to start conversations and *where* to go to meet people. This concern was echoed in studies conducted recently by Zimbardo and his colleagues at Stanford which indicate that over 40 percent of college students experience uncomfortable shyness in interpersonal situations. A search of the literature revealed a lack of material that offered step-by-step guidelines for changing social behavior and a way to evaluate your progress. This book provides such guidelines as well as exercises to help you assess your progress. It deals with how *you* can take action in your social contacts.

Encouraging people to take a more active role in achieving more satisfying social exchanges is certainly not new. What is new is the technology of "self-management" that has become available to aid you in this endeavor. You'll find the steps involved in this process in the Introduction.

The full value of the procedures we describe in the book will only be realized insofar as you apply them as recommended. You of course may pick up some useful ideas just browsing through the manual, but such an approach will not allow the full effect. The difficult aspect of any self-improvement program is getting yourself to *do* things. (We all know what happens to well-intentioned New Year's Resolutions.) The self-management techniques which are built into the manual will help you over these hurdles; however you have to take action in carrying them out. With this in mind, we think you should ask yourself whether you are really serious, that is, willing to expend some effort in trying to improve the quality of your social life.

It's Up to You is also the title of a videotape on assertion training for women produced at Berkeley, in which we stress the active role one *must* play in order to increase social contacts. Assertion training, as first stressed by Andrew Salter and then by Joseph Wolpe, emphasizes the value of expressing negative and positive feelings in social interaction. The material in this manual deals mainly with situations calling for *positive assertion*, such as initiating contacts and arranging future meetings, although we do discuss negative assertion as it is relevant to enjoyable social contact. We also encourage you to increase the risks

7

you take in social interactions as well as show you how to regulate these risks through the development of skills for coping with interfering thoughts and feelings.

We are indebted to many investigators and writers and have listed those to whom credit is especially due in the bibliography. Also we owe a great debt to the many men and women who have participated in our assertion training groups and who have offered us valuable suggestions and feedback.

A study we carried out at the University of California in Berkeley with a group of women aged 19 to 34, including both students and non-students, has shown that this manual *can* indeed be helpful in increasing the frequency and enjoyment of social contacts. However, it can only be really effective if you do the step-by-step exercises as suggested. We welcome feedback as to what you find especially useful in the manual as well as which areas you had difficulty with so that we may improve future editions of the book.

Introduction

Perhaps one of the most frequent complaints by adults is that they do not have as many enjoyable social contacts as they would like. How can those who feel this need fulfill it? By changing their behavior to expand their social opportunities. The specific changes required will vary from person to person. You may need to develop skills such as how and where to meet people, and how to arrange future meetings. Or, you may wish to learn how to participate more in conversations, how to disagree successfully with others and how to maintain more enjoyable conversations. Most of us can benefit from cultivating a more adventurous attitude in social encounters, one in which risks are more willingly accepted because we see the possible benefits involved.

This book is organized so that you can consider your individual needs. In addition to a series of core chapters which all readers are encouraged to read, there are chapters relating to specific behaviors, thoughts or feelings—how to increase your participation in conversations, how to disagree with others, how to decrease negative thoughts related to social encounters—which you need read only if they are relevant to your interests.

It is important to be assertive in your social relations to maximize returns. People can and should be active in the construction of their own social environments—just waiting around and being patient is not likely to expose you to rewarding contacts. In the chapters which follow you'll learn where to go to meet people; when to approach a person; what to say; how to handle a negative response. You'll find out how to maintain an encounter that is mutually enjoyable. Other important skills outlined include being able to disagree with tact, achieving *conversational reciprocity* by balancing talking with listening; being able to handle (or redirect) a boring conversation; and being able to express your own ideas and feelings. The techniques covered are particularly helpful for people who wish to enlarge their circle of acquaintances and thereby expand their choices.

The book also provides information on how to increase contacts with those you already know so that those who are now acquaintances may become good friends; or they may develop into a romantic involvement. Although the purpose of this book is not to serve as a guide for how to transform a relationship into a love affair, once you accept responsibility for your social life many possibilities will arise. It is, however, first necessary to learn how to interact successfully during *early* contacts. Still, many of the areas discussed are as relevant to the maintenance of enjoyable long-term relationships as to establishing new ones—learning how to express disagreements, learning how to say no, arranging enjoyable activities to share together.

Although this manual is primarily intended to be used without professional guidance, it would also be a useful supplement to individual or group counseling which focuses upon interpersonal skill development. If you suffer severe anxiety in social situations, professional help is recommended either as a prelude to, or together with, use of this manual. If you find that you are unable to identify needed changes, such help is also recommended.

The guidelines presented are for both women and men. Many women may still believe that men desire a submissive, acquiescent woman; however, many men actually prefer a woman who is independent and self-assertive. More important, of course, is deciding what type of person *you* want to be. Women have every right and even a responsibility to take the initiative in establishing social contacts. It can be a burden for a man to always have to be responsible for initiating contacts, keeping things interesting, and making suggestions. Mutual effort contributes to mutual respect and equality. Women must play a more active role in social relations so that true reciprocity can occur.

A Technique of Self-management

The material presented in this book rests upon a number of assumptions:

- **A technology of behavior is available which can help us change our own behavior, that is, self-management is possible.** The last two decades have witnessed the application of social learning principles to an increasingly wide variety of areas including parent-child and marital interaction, assertive behavior, anxiety reactions, and depression. In the course of such applications, a technology has emerged with guidelines on how to apply these principles. There is now evidence that people can learn to be their *own* managers of behavior change. That is essentially what this manual will involve you in doing. It will offer you the information and procedures necessary to bring about change. But you will be the one to actually carry out the steps in the program and evaluate your own progress.

- **Most of our behavior is learned and is a function of its consequences.** The principles upon which the technology of behavior is based rest upon the repeated findings that behavior is a function of its consequences. Thus if you wish to increase the frequency of someone's behavior, you should arrange for positive consequences to be associated with that behavior. For example, if you want to increase another person's pleasant statements, you would *reinforce* these each time s(he) said something you thought was pleasant. A *positive reinforcer* is anything that increases or strengthens the behavior which it follows such as praise, smiles, or your attention. (These are *social reinforcers*—those consequences which consist of another person's behavior.)

If, on the other hand, you wish to decrease a behavior, you should arrange for a lack of rewarding effects or even for an unpleasant one. If you would like to cut off a very talkative person who is monopolizing the conversation for instance, you should stop smiling or nodding in agreement, or showing any sign of interest. You could also turn away or look at your watch. The talkative behavior is very likely to decrease.

These principles describe relationships between behavior and environmental events. They are laws that have been discovered to operate. Science does not know *why* they operate, only that they do, and that they affect our behavior whether or not we recognize their influence. Also these laws of behavior are never suspended in time; they are always at work whether we think about them or not.

- **Behavior must be specified before it can be changed.** You are probably in the habit of using vague general terms to describe changes you would like to bring about. You may say to yourself, "I wish I was a different type of person," without going on to ask, "What would I *do* if I were a different type of person?" In this book, you will be asked to specify what it would mean for you to "meet more people." You will identify the types of people you want to meet, under what circumstances, and how frequently you would like social contacts of varying durations. You will also learn to pinpoint the specific behaviors necessary to change in order to increase these contacts.

  Unless you are clear about exactly what you want, change is unlikely. This can lead to a feeling of hopelessness about ever being able to exert more control over your environment. In essence, we cannot change something unless we know *what* it is we wish to change.

- **Behavior is most comfortably and successfully changed in a step-by-step fashion.** Once objectives have been identified, comfortable change often requires the completion of intermediate steps, gradually leading to your final objectives. Let's say you want to increase how often you compliment others, (an effective means of maintaining more enjoyable conversations). The first steps would be to find out how often you compliment others right now and to set a reasonable goal to increase this amount. Perhaps you do not compliment others at all. Your first objective might be to increase this to one time during each conversation which is at least five minutes long. Then perhaps you would like to expand the number of ways in which you compliment someone, varying from those that are easy for you to say to those that are more difficult. It may be easier for you to compliment a person on his appearance than to tell him you think he is a nice person. The immediate goal would be to start with compliments which are just slightly difficult and, as you become comfortable with these, practice the next most difficult one, and so on.

One attitude that interferes with change is the expectation that we should be able to reach a goal quickly without much effort. You may say I am interested in finding someone with whom I can form a deep love relationship. Or, I am interested in getting to know some people who are doing very interesting things. Even if you already have the skills required to obtain these objectives, access may require many steps—meeting new people, finding out how they live and what they think about. You may have to interact with many people before you find someone you find very interesting or with whom you can form a lasting intimate relationship. The way to make the whole process more pleasurable is to make these intermediate steps reinforcing in and of themselves, not solely as a means toward an end. Specific ways to accomplish this are described in the manual.

- **We learn by doing.** Many people try to reach decisions and change behavior by only thinking or talking about change. When only thought and talk are involved, there is no practice of desired behaviors and no feedback is provided as to progress. Are things really getting better or worse? Thus, doing not only provides practice but also feedback about our behavior.

- **Behavior should be monitored.** Trying to change behavior without evaluating the degree of change can be falsely discouraging. Only by keeping track of what we do can we determine whether a particular behavior or thought is occurring more or less freqeuntly. Let's say you wish to increase the frequency with which you offer opinions when talking to others. You first select some convenient time period and count how often you now express opinions when talking to others. You could then set a reachable goal, acquire any new behaviors which are necessary to accomplish this, and continue to occasionally note how often you offer opinions after you try to increase these. This will let you know whether your efforts are successful.

How To Use This Manual

All readers are urged to read Chapters 1 through 10. A brief overview of these chapters is presented below. Other chapters are to be read on an "as needed" basis dependent upon what specific behaviors, thoughts, and feelings you feel you should address in order to increase enjoyable social exchanges. Successful use of the manual requires your active participation in carrying out recommended tasks. These tasks incorporate the following requirements for bringing about change: identification of goals and the changes required to reach these; selection of a way to alter your behavior in a step-by-step fashion to achieve these changes; and arrangement for feedback as to how you are doing.

To help you understand some of the reasons you have not been more successful or more active in achieving enjoyable social contacts, read over the "stumbling blocks" to determine which pertain to you. You should then set goals by deciding *who* you wish to increase contacts with; how to gather and record is discussed in Chapter 2. You are asked to "globally" describe the types of people you would like to see more of. The use of the word *global* here is deliberate since people often miss opportunities for enjoyable social contacts by being *too* selective in who they initiate contacts with. They may misjudge and lose out on meeting an interesting person. Chapters 2 and 3 offer you ways to assess your current social behavior. You are asked to observe certain characteristics of your social encounters for a one week period—methods are offered to make this observation as easy as possible. Chapter 2 also shows you how to use the information you collect to develop assignments as well as indicates what other chapters will be most useful to read. This will help you select behaviors, thoughts or feelings you should alter—such as increasing the frequency with which you express your ideas and feelings (Chapter 11), learning how to disagree with others (Chapter 13) or learning how to decrease anxiety related to social situations (Chapter 15). Suggestions for practicing and becoming comfortable with new behavior are presented in Chapter 3. Guidelines for selecting assignments are in Chapter 4. Sample assignments are presented at the end of each chapter where relevant.

Chapter 5 offers guidelines for self-reinforcement and Chapter 6 discusses how to keep track of what is happening so you will be able to evaluate your progress and know when to select more difficult assignments. Suggestions for scanning your own environment to locate places where you can meet others are discussed in Chapter 7. Different ways to initiate conversations are presented in Chapter 8. You will find guidelines for maintaining conversations, for ending discussions and for arranging future meetings in Chapters 9 and 10. Chapters 11 through 15 deal with specific behaviors, thoughts, and feelings that relate to enjoyable social contacts. For example, you may not use skills you already have due to anxiety in certain social situations. You may worry that you are boring, will be rejected, or are not an interesting person. How to handle such troublesome thoughts and the anxiety associated with them is dealt with in Chapters 14 and 15.

A typical change program may include the following steps: (1) gradually increasing the frequency with which you *initiate* exchanges with people you are interested in; (2) gradually increasing the *duration* of these contacts; (3) arranging *more* brief meetings; (4) increasing the frequency with which you arrange for *longer* meetings. The assessment information you gather during your exchanges with people will help you to identify other behaviors you should work on to enhance enjoyable conversations. These might include increasing the frequency with which you express your ideas and feelings or learning how to effectively disagree with others. You will gradually change your behavior by carrying out assignments in accord with your skill and comfort levels.

1

Stumbling Blocks to Successful Social Contacts

It is very likely that the explanation for why you are not more active or more successful in making social contacts is among the following:

- I don't like to go alone

- I don't know how to act or what to do

- I am too busy

- I am too lazy

- I never meet anyone interesting

- I am too self-conscious

- I don't know any suitable places to go

- I rely on chance meetings

- I am afraid of getting turned down

- I resent having to make the effort

It is important to recognize those which pertain to you since any one can interfere with developing enjoyable relationships. Many of the sections in the book address these interferences; thus, going over this chapter will give you an overview. You should carefully read the sections of the book which relate to you.

• **I don't like to go alone** This is a common reason put forth for not engaging in assertive social behavior. You may not think that it is proper to be seen alone in public situations, that is you feel pressure to go with a friend or escort. Whether it is really acceptable to go places alone depends upon the situation. It is perfectly acceptable to go alone to concerts, classes, or discussion groups. You should also consider the time of day, day of the week, how many others are present and the activities that occur. Until you feel free to go anywhere at anytime, it

15

might be helpful to take advantage of situations where this freedom already exists. Art galleries, classrooms, libraries, stores and museums are examples of places where it is as acceptable for a woman or a man to go alone as it is to be accompanied by someone else.

Another reason you may not like to go out alone is that you may think that you will be considered unpopular or desperate. You may even see *yourself* as undesirable when you go unescorted. This attitude obviously limits your freedom; your fear of social criticism causes you to miss opportunities. This fear can be diminished if you first select those situations in which you feel fairly comfortable and then gradually go on to more difficult situations. For example, you might first attend events such as concerts, where you are one of many observers. As you experience more comfort in going out alone, you could begin to attend events where you are slightly more conspicuous since there are fewer people. As it becomes more common for you to be among people by yourself at a variety of functions, your expectation of criticism for being there alone will gradually decrease. Also as more people assume this attitude the possibility of criticism is reduced for everyone. Thus, by going places alone when you feel like it, you not only increase your range of freedom, but also help to increase it for others as well. It is also possible you may not like to go places alone since you are afraid of being attacked, or mugged. This fear may be realistic in some areas, especially at night. If so, you can arrange to go places for the most part during the day, or only to places in the less dangerous neighborhoods—you could take a taxi or go with a friend or acquaintance. The point is that if you really want to go where it is possible to meet people, a safe acceptable way can be found to do so, given that you spend a bit of time to identify an appropriate place and way to get there.

• **I don't know how to act or what to do**   You may not go to places to meet people because you do not have the skills that make such activity productive and enjoyable. Once there you may tend to stay to yourself, not knowing when to get involved or how. In Chapters 8 through 10 you'll find guidelines and examples of how to deal with this problem—how to initiate conversations with others, how to maintain them, and how to end them and arrange future meetings. In addition, guidelines are presented as to where to first comfortably try out these skills and how to work up to more difficult situations after you have had successful experiences. With increased skills and self-assurance, you will feel more comfortable making initial overtures rather than playing a passive role.

Another problem in knowing what to do in social contacts may be that you don't have the skills and self-assurance to handle unpleasant responses from others. That is, you may avoid exposing yourself to situations in which you can meet new people and avoid conversations once there, because you do not know how to react to sarcastic or negative remarks. Chapter 8 especially deals with how these can be handled and offers concrete examples so you need not fear embarrassment or rejection. Once you develop a less sensitive attitude and learn how to react to negative responses you will feel more free in exchanges with others since you are not preoccupied with the possibility of a negative outcome.

• **I am too busy**   Many people feel they are too busy to make the necessary effort to meet people because they don't organize their time to their best advantage. If you work and have a family, serious planning of activities is required so that you have some time for yourself. This planning may involve arranging for child care, dividing up household chores among family members, and finding places to go that do not require a long trip. Many married women place everyone else's interests over their own rather than realize that they count as much as other family members. Some women feel guilty about leaving their children with a babysitter while they do something they enjoy. This is unfortunate for both the woman and her children. If a woman deprives herself of social contacts and other enjoyable activities which are important to any adult, she may begin to resent her children, and make them suffer for her own unhappiness. Also it is beneficial for children to relate to other adults, such as babysitters, and to come to realize that they cannot be totally dependent upon their mother for the satisfaction of all their needs and desires.

Another factor in the "too busy" category applies to those who may not have the energy at the end of the day to engage in social activities. This again can be dealt with by planning. You may want to limit your social activities to the weekends when you have more energy. You could organize child care so that you would be freed from the routine feeding and bedtime activities at least once a week; friends could take turns doing these activities. An arrangement could be made between friends or between a husband and a wife to share child care chores so that some time is provided to pursue other social contacts. If you are single and work very long hours and then complain that you never meet anyone, it is probably because you do not devote the time necessary to do so. You must decide whether you are really serious about meeting more people, and if so then arrange your schedule accordingly. The guidelines presented in the manual will help you to select those situations which are most likely to produce enjoyable encounters, thus saving the amount of time you have to commit to this endeavor. No matter what your situation, if you want to, you can arrange your activities so that you will have time.

• **I am too lazy** This attitude indicates that you probably should reward yourself more for engaging in social activities. If you are not in the habit of going places it may be necessary for you to offer yourself something every time you engage in an activity related to making social contacts. In time the activities themselves will become so rewarding that participation in them will be sufficient to maintain your behavior. The book's stress upon selecting activities which you enjoy and which offer the greatest opportunity for meeting others, will also reduce the difficulty you may have in getting yourself going.

Saying "I'm too lazy" may also indicate that you really don't like interacting with others all that much. If you decide that you want to meet more people, you must learn how to obtain more enjoyment from social interactions and sections of the manual are devoted to this.

• **I never meet anyone interesting** If this is an explanation you give for not getting out to meet people and interacting with them, it may be that you have been disappointed in the past. This disappointment may result from the fact that you did not meet "fascinating" people right away. You could be overly selective about who you interact with. You should allow yourself and the other person a chance to sample enough behavior to know whether further interaction would be enjoyable. For example, if you are only interested in finding a mate, all other positive values of interacting with others may seem disappointing. If this is the case, you are depriving yourself of a variety of positive social encounters as well as cutting off opportunities for meeting a mate. You may actually prematurely cut off contact with a potential partner or friend because you are not skilled in bringing out another person so that s(he) does become interesting to you.

It may also be that you often get "stuck" with one person at social gatherings and don't know how to break away tactfully and meet other more interesting people. Specific examples of how to terminate conversations and guidelines for making conversations more interesting and enjoyable are presented in Chapters 11 through 14.

• **I am too self-conscious** You may not go places to meet people because you feel unattractive or awkward in public situations. Worrying what others will think about you can lead to anxiety which interferes with an appropriate display of your social assets. Negative thoughts are identified and procedures are described for decreasing their frequency and for increasing the frequency of positive thoughts in Chapter 15. This will help you to be more relaxed in social situations and increase the possibility for your contacts to be successful.

• **I don't know any suitable places to go** You may already be in situations where it is highly possible to meet people, such as classes and work, once you learn to recognize and take advantage of these opportunities. To cultivate additional opportunities it is important to start with places where you feel fairly comfortable and then work up to more difficult ones. Guidelines are presented to help you do this.

• **I rely on chance meetings**   You may be under the impression that people you meet by sheer chance are somehow more desirable than those you meet via some planned activity like a discussion group. Actually, there is no evidence to support this notion. In fact those you meet in the course of an activity which interests you are more likely to be responsive to you because of shared interests. You must decide to exercise more control over your life if you want to improve your social contacts.

• **I am afraid of being turned down**   If you don't attempt to initiate contacts because you fear being rejected it is likely that you are overemphasizing the "cost" in one direction. You may be dwelling on the effects of possible rejections rather than seeing the limitations imposed on your behavior and enjoyment by your fear and consequent failure to act. Certainly if you lack the skills to achieve effective social behavior, you may have received so many negative reactions that you decided to be passive. This manual is designed to help you develop these skills so you can experience more comfort and enjoyment in social interactions because your overtures are followed by positive reactions from others. On the other hand you may at times receive a negative or harsh reply for a variety of other reasons. The person may be preoccupied, tired or just in a "bad mood;" they might snap at you, ignore you, or even ridicule you. When you have mastered the skills detailed in the book you will be able to take reactions like these in your stride.

• **I resent having to make the effort**   Perhaps you think that meeting interesting people should just happen without special effort on your part. Or you may be in a new situation where you have to start meeting people after many years of secure social relationships (you have moved, lost a lover, are divorced, widowed or changed jobs). If this is the case you have to decide whether meeting people is important enough to warrant some extra attention and effort. Another attitude that may lie behind resenting the effort is that you do not anticipate that the steps involved in new social exchanges will be pleasurable. The manual describes a variety of ways to make the whole process more efficient and effective, as well as more enjoyable.

The next chapter will show you how to assess your goals in light of your current social behavior and how to identify the general types of contacts you wish to increase.

2

Setting Goals

What Would You Like to Achieve?

An important step in changing behavior is identifying the ways in which you would like things to be different. Space is provided below for you to indicate the general kinds of interactions you would like to have more frequently as well as those you would not. This will help you to identify what you should keep track of at this stage of assessment. You are also asked to indicate how often you would like to have brief, intermediate, and extended contacts.

Contact Goals

I would like to have more contacts with:

sex: men_____ women_____ both men and women _____

age: people my own age_____ older_____ younger_____
doesn't matter_____

relationship: Strangers_____ acquaintances_____ both_____

Exceptions   Individuals you do not wish to increase contacts with (specify):

roommates_____

friends_____

people at work_____

others_____

How often would you like to have in-person social contacts?

	Brief*	Intermediate**	Extended***
1. Daily	_____	_____	_____
2. Every other day	_____	_____	_____
3. One or two times a week	_____	_____	_____
4. Every other week	_____	_____	_____
5. Once a month	_____	_____	_____

*More than just a greeting but under 15 minutes.
**Between 16 minutes and an hour
***Over one hour

20

Taking a Look at Your Current Behavior

Where you start your behavior change program depends upon what you do at the present time. Thus, a first step is to observe your behavior and record what you find. This will require some effort on your part since you are asked to keep track of given aspects of your conduct. You simply observe specific behaviors and thoughts and record these observations. During this assessment phase you will find it helpful to note several aspects of your social behavior for a one-week period. Pertinent information concerning your contacts should be marked down as soon as possible after your meetings; waiting until the end of the day might distort your data. Try to continue acting as you normally would during this time so that you can gather an accurate picture of your current social behavior. If some of the days during which you record are atypical—you go on a trip or perhaps become ill—and do not provide an accurate picture of your social contacts, you should record for additional days until you reach a total of seven. (Be sure to include a weekend as well as weekdays.) To record this data effectively use checklists A and B which are in the Appendix. (Feel free to tear out Appendix pages for your use—make additional copies as needed.)

Keeping Track of Your Social Contacts

Side one of Checklist A (See Appendix A) is to be used to note actual conversations you have which are more than just a greeting (a simple statement or question) with individuals with whom you wish to *increase* contact. (Do not record information about other contacts you may have on this side.) Thus, if you wish to have more interactions with men only, you will record only these conversations. If you want to increase the number of contacts you have solely with men outside of work, you would note only these interactions. Do not record exchanges which are *strictly* of a service or business nature. For example, discussing food with a grocer, or asking a salesperson to show you furniture or a librarian where a book might be found would not be considered social contacts. However, if you ask a salesperson to show you furniture and then proceed to discuss related personal topics, such as your taste in furniture or the salesperson's opinions, then this elaborated exchange would be considered social contact which you should record *if* the person is one with whom you wish to increase your contacts.

When it is relevant note whether the situation involved a man or woman by indicating M or F in the column under sex. Other abbreviations are explained on the checklist. On the reverse side of Checklist A note situations in which you *could* have started a conversation but did not. You should use Checklist A to keep track of your social contacts both during assessment and after you try to increase them.

Making Use of the Information You Collect

Keeping track of your social contacts on Checklist A for the first week will make you aware of whether your current interactions involve people you want to see more of and whether you are meeting new people. Noting where your contacts take place will inform you as to the range of situations in which you are meeting people. Checklist A also provides other information of value such as how you think others respond to you; how you initiate conversations; how long your contacts tend to be; and how much you enjoy your social exchanges. Each bit of information can help you understand how to profitably change your behavior in order to increase your social contacts. (Subsequent Checklist A records will keep you in touch with how you are progressing in increasing the number and enjoyment of your contacts.)

Assessing Your Contacts

After you have monitored your contacts for the first seven-day period compare the number of contacts you actually have had and the number you said you would like to have as a *contact goal*. If there is little or no difference, then either you underestimate your current success in your social contacts or keeping track of your behavior has had an effect on it. To confirm the latter point, once again without attempting to change your behavior, record your social contacts for another week on Checklist A. The main decision you have to make at this point is whether you really want to have more social contacts than you now have.

Did you initiate any contacts?   If you did not initiate many of the contacts you had during this week, you obviously should focus on taking a more active role when meeting others. Chapter 8 "How To Initiate Conversations" presents a variety of methods which you should find helpful and feel comfortable with. Also the chapters on "Maintaining Conversations" and "How To Have Enjoyable Conversations" will be of further benefit.

Did others initiate conversations with you?   In addition to learning how to take a more active part in making social contacts it might also prove profitable to examine your behavior to see whether you are as open as you could be in relation to encouraging others to initiate contacts with you. If your Checklist A indicates a low frequency of other people initiating contacts with you, you should find it helpful to read the sections on how to encourage initiations from others in Chapter 8.

Where did you meet people?   Based on Checklist A, indicate the total number of different places you went where it was *possible* for you to meet people you would like to see more frequently, and also the number in which you made verbal contact with such people.

1. Total number of different places I went where it was possible to meet people _____
2. Number in which I actually met someone _____

If there is a large difference between (1) and (2), then you apparently do not take advantage of the opportunities for meeting people you are interested in. If you do not have many places numbered in (1), then you are not seeking out places where it is likely that you can meet such individuals and you will have to arrange to do so. Or, it could be that you are misjudging the possibilities in these situations and that you really could meet people you would like in these contexts. Guidelines for the selection of places to meet people and how to take advantage of the situation are presented in Chapter 7 "Where To Go To Meet People."

The Situation Summary Sheet located in Appendix B will help you assess whether you are seeking out places where there are actual opportunities to meet people. (Use Checklist A to obtain the information for this summary.) List only the different *types* of situations where you had social contacts. For example, if you find that you started three conversations during the week and all of them were on the bus, then you list only *one* type of situation—*"on the bus."* As you begin practicing the guidelines described in the manual particularly those in Chapter 7, you should be able to find more situations in which you initiate contacts such as in the market, at a party, even standing in a theater line.

Did you enjoy the conversations? If you think you could have enjoyed your contacts more turn to Chapter 12, "How To Have More Enjoyable Conversations" and try out some of the recommendations. Also take a careful look at Checklist B described in the next section of this chapter to identify behaviors, thoughts, or feelings you have when interacting with others that might hinder your enjoyment.

How do you think others responded to you? Look over Checklist A and see how you judged other people's reactions to you. If your judgment was that most were positive, this is at least an indication that most of the time you feel good about other people's reaction to exchanges with you. If you indicated that the reactions were often negative, use Checklist B in the Appendix to identify behaviors, thoughts, and/or feelings that may interfere with your own spontaneity and performance in social exchanges and which may limit the other person's enjoyment.

It is also possible that you are incorrect in your judgment of whether or not people have enjoyed their exchanges with you. As you acquire the skills outlined you will have more concrete criteria by which to assess others' reactions when interacting with you.

Keeping a daily log   In addition to Checklist A you may want to keep a notebook where each day you record relevant behaviors, thoughts or feelings. It will be helpful if you indicate where you were and who was involved so that you can identify the contexts in which you have difficulty.

Examples of entries:

2/1   Waiting for the bus. Felt like starting a conversation with the man standing next to me but did not.

2/1   At work. Thought of saying hello to new person when I saw him standing by the water cooler but did not.

2/1   Coming home sitting on bus. Felt like starting a conversation with the woman sitting next to me but did not.

The information on this log will be especially helpful in completing future checklists to assess your progress.

Interaction Summary

This form (Appendix C) is provided for you to keep track of your social behavior on a weekly basis over an extended period of time. There is space to note each week that you monitor your behavior. The next column is labeled AEL for average enjoyment level. To find this figure add the numbers in the Checklist A *ENJOYMENT* column and divide by the number of entries.

In the next column, record the total number of contacts you had during each week. Notice that space is also provided for the separate notation of number of contacts with strangers and acquaintances and men and women. Space is provided to note the number of contacts of various durations since you probably will want to increase the number of longer interactions that you have. This form will provide a ready source of feedback on your progress during the program. You can also use this information to select appropriate behavior assignments.

Identifying Behavior Which Affects Pleasurable Contacts

Checklist B (see Appendix D) can be used to identify which behaviors and thoughts have a negative or positive effect on your longer exchanges. Select two interactions from Checklist A, one which was especially pleasant and one which was especially unpleasant and complete a separate Checklist B for each of these as soon as possible after your exchange. The items on this checklist were selected for their relationship to enjoyable social exchanges. On the reverse side you are asked to answer four additional items; try to be as specific as possible in completing these. For instance, in recording a pleasant impression of someone rather than noting merely "he was nice," write down what made you decide he was nice. He might have smiled frequently, listened when you spoke or asked you relevant questions about what you said. In judging the strength of your own performance an example might be that you asked a person for his opinion on a number of occasions. Finally, you are requested to record specific behaviors, thoughts, or feelings that you would like to increase or decrease. For example, perhaps you now are constantly aware of feeling tense and your goal may be to feel more relaxed.

After you complete the items on the back of Checklist B, scan them to make sure they are specific. For each item ask, "Could I identify this behavior, thought or feeling later if I were asked to?" For instance, could you actually count the number of times you disagreed when you felt like it, the amount of time someone listened to you and the number or relevant questions asked. The reason for the stress upon specifically identifying what occurs is so you can be as clear as possible as to what you should do more or less of to increase the number of enjoyable exchanges that you have.

Making Use of Checklist B

Look over the first page of the Checklist B sheets you filled out during the week and see whether you found any negative items listed there occurring frequently. Did you worry about what the other person was thinking when you were talking to him or her? Did you feel tense during the conversation? Did you worry that you would run out of things to say? If you found any of these troublesome feelings prevalent, turn to the appropriate section of the manual and read the instructions contained in that section. Try to use the methods described there to change the troublesome behavior. Specific behaviors which you noted on the reverse side of Checklist B under Item 4 can be used as an additional guide to identify negative areas and their positive counterparts.

The most effective way to change behaviors is to concentrate upon increasing appropriate, rather than upon decreasing inappropriate ones. Thus, the emphasis in the manual will be on positive behavior and thoughts that will make your interactions more frequent and more enjoyable.

Your answers to Item 3, which asks you to record strengths in your own performance, should help you to identify things you do that you would like to increase. Remember to identify behaviors in a very definitive way. Your answers to Item 2 will help you to identify specific things that others say or do that "turns you off." (If you cannot specify what it is that you dislike about a person it is difficult to attempt to change it, either by encouraging alternative behavior, or by talking about it with the person.) Finally a review of Item 1, which requests you to identify interesting or pleasant things about the other person, will make it possible for you to offer support via compliments and attention as described in Chapter 12.

Assertion Inventory

You should also find it helpful to complete the Assertion Inventory located in Appendix E. This includes a number of situations which are topics of focus within the manual. After you complete the inventory, you should note those items which you indicated cause you high discomfort and/or which have a low response probability. For example, if you indicate high discomfort to Item 26, "Expressing an opinion that differs from that of the person you are talking to," you should benefit from learning new ways of introducing opinion statements (in Chapter 11) and disagreeing with others (Chapter 13) and should try out the procedures described. Look over the inventory for any areas of difficulty and read the appropriate chapters.

3

Rehearsal and Assessment

When working on troublesome areas you are encouraged to assess your behavior via rehearsal before you try out new actions in real situations. This will help you to find out whether your response is OK as is or whether there is room for improvement. If you find there is room for improvement you must decide what to do differently and practice to develop skill and comfort with the new behavior. You should practice until you feel comfortable with the idea of trying it out, and feel confident that success is likely in actual situations.

Role Playing

When you are rehearsing (role playing) to find out what to do differently or to develop skill in a new behavior *be specific about the situation*. For example, if you want to increase the frequency with which you offer opinion statements, there are undoubtedly some people with whom you would feel more comfortable asserting yourself in this specific manner than in other assertive situations.

In addition, practicing new techniques in the least anxiety-provoking situations will provide a better opportunity for you to discover appropriate behaviors. You are more likely to say the "right thing" when you are less anxious. Let's say you feel little discomfort expressing an opinion about a movie you have seen when you are talking to someone of the same sex; more discomfort if discussing this with someone of the opposite sex; and a great deal of discomfort with someone of the opposite sex who you found very attractive. You should start by assessing your skills in the first situation. You may find that your basic skills are very adequate, you merely need to practice them in more difficult situations. That is, you do not have to learn a *new* behavior, just to become more comfortable using those skills you already have. Rehearsal can accomplish this. It is helpful to write down each problem situation on a separate card, then rate each item in terms of subjective anxiety (have zero = calm to 100 = very anxious) and order these in terms of how much discomfort each induces. You can then start with the easiest situations first. The script cards in Appendix F can be used for this purpose.

Another important thing to do in behavior rehearsal is to be sure to *engage in constructive criticism*. For example, if you are trying to assess how you sound when you start conversations, record some opening statements on audio-tape, play it back and focus on what you did *well* as well as what you could do *differently* to improve your effectiveness. Reinforce yourself for effective behavior you already possess in addition to working for improvement. Since you are learning new behaviors and how to be comfortable with them, it is expected that there will be a need for improvement.

Finding Out What To Do Differently

Let's say that you have role-played a situation and feel there is room for improvement. How do you find out what to do differently? First, you yourself may be able to identify what you should do differently. Your notes on Checklist B may help you to select which specific behaviors to change. The examples provided in the chapters should further help you identify what to increase and what to decrease.

In addition, it is often helpful to observe others who behave successfully, being sure to select models who act assertively, with ease and comfort, and avoiding models who are submissive or aggressive. The people you choose to watch don't have to be live models. You can also learn from observing peole on TV and in the movies. Assertive behavior is defined as the open expression of one's preferences in such a way that others take them into account, whereas aggressive behavior is defined as the hostile expression of preferences in such a way that others give in to them. Aggressive actions or words take away the rights of others, in contrast to assertive behavior which serves to maintain one's own just rights. Submissive behavior, on the other hand, permits one's rights to be ignored and is seen in yielding humbly, apologetically, to the preferences of others. Each of us has a right to express assertive social behaviors. If you have difficulty disagreeing with others for example, watch people who disagree assertively with ease and success and notice specifically what they do and say. It is helpful to write it down so that you will remember these later as you practice. (Try to make your notes specific.) No doubt you will observe some of the behaviors mentioned in the manual and can see how these can be successfully employed in real situations.

Once you have a picture of what to do, you can practice using one of the methods described below. Learning new behaviors and becoming more comfortable with them whether old or new, is easier if you progress in small steps, from easy to more difficult ones. Practice any one step until you have mastered it before moving on.

A variety of ways to practice new behaviors is described below. Select a method that provides helpful feedback and which is successful in gradually decreasing any discomfort you may feel.

Practicing Verbal Skills

If you wish to increase your ability to initiate conversations, you should first read Chapter 8 and select one or two ways in which you feel you could be more successful. You could practice the behavior, that is, talk outloud, using your own perception of how you sound as a guide to what could be improved. Remember to be precise concerning the context of the exchange. You may have to role-play asking someone for a future meeting, you may want to practice asking different people as well as prepare yourself for a variety of reactions ranging from positive acceptances, polite refusals to snappy turn downs. You might find it much easier to handle a polite refusal than a sharp one. If so, start your practice with the former and when you feel comfortable with this and know what is appropriate to say, then rehearse your reaction to a more negative reply.

You could record yourself on audiotape and then play it back and identify what you do that is appropriate and the specific ways in which you could improve. Do you speak loudly enough? Does your voice sound flat or lively? Does the affect expressed in your voice match what you say? Do you speak fluently? Is the content OK? You might ask a friend to offer helpful feedback and to role-play situations with you. Only select this method if your partner can offer you constructive criticism, or if s(he) can simply carry out the reciprocal role without any feedback. Avoid the partner who is overly eager to provide you with scores of helpful hints if these overwhelm you, or one who feels it's her duty to tell you how inept you are.

You could also practice the behavior; that is imagine yourself or an effective model in a situation, and imagine what happens. Close your eyes when imagining scenes so that you shut out distracting events. Try to imagine all important details of the situation as clearly as possible. Where does it take place? What does the person look like with whom you are interacting? What do you look like during this exchange? What does he say? What do you feel? Imagine varying reactions to your statement starting with a scene which is fairly easy for you to imagine handling successfully.

Another way to rehearse is to record scenes on tape, being sure to describe all important details, and listen to each one while imagining the situation and what is said and done. It is more effective to imagine a scene in which you experience initial anxiety and overcome this (a coping response) than to imagine that no anxiety is present at all (a mastery response).

If you experience no anxiety at all when you imagine a scene, it could indicate that you are not imagining the situation clearly enough. The effectiveness of this procedure is related to the clarity of scenes. Give yourself time to imagine a scene as clearly as possible. These covert procedures are most valuable if practiced as described. Whatever method you select, rehearse the behavior until you feel that you know how to do it and feel fairly comfortable with the idea of trying it out in a real life situation. You may have to practice one behavior a number of times. Do not overburden yourself by trying to do too much. You should probably select only one or two behaviors to practice at any one time.

Practicing Body Language

You can practice nonverbal behaviors (gestures, eye contact, posture, facial expression) and receive feedback about how you look by practicing in front of a mirror. For example, if you wonder how open you look to conversation when with others, place yourself in front of a mirror. Close your eyes and imagine a specific situation as clearly as possible. It helps to be dressed as you would be in the situation. If you try to assess your body language while initiating conversations in your pajamas, this may throw you off because of the disparity of your dress. Try to position your body as you think you typically appear. Then open your eyes and critically examine how you look. Remember, the criticism should be constructive. Try to identify what you like and pinpoint behavior that could be improved. Do not engage in useless general negative statements. Ask yourself the following check questions: Do your eyes appear welcoming? Is there the hint of a smile around your mouth or do you look tense or unpleasant? Are your arms relaxed or are they tensed and unnatural looking? Ask yourself honestly, if you saw someone who looked as you do, would you be interested in starting a conversation with him or her? If the answer is no or questionable, try to identify ways in which you could appear more open to conversation.

After you have identified some nonverbal behaviors to change, practice in front of the mirror until you are satisfied with how you behave. Some people have the idea that it is vain to look into mirrors; however, mirrors show us how we appear to others and can be used as an aid to improving the way we behave.

Sample Assignments

For the next three days, observe how other people initiate conversations and write down what they do that is effective.

Select three different situations in which you would like to initiate a conversation and record your response, on a tape recorder, one at a time starting with a situation in which you feel fairly comfortable. Listen to your statements and select two things that you do that are useful and two things you could do differently to be more successful.

Practice offering opinion statements with different degrees of voice volume (loudness) and with different pause patterns. Record these statements and listen to them. Identify the best loudness of voice and the pause pattern you think is most effective and practice these.

Ask a friend how s(he) disagrees with other people and ask them to model a couple of these ways for you. Select two verbal or nonverbal components of his or her reactions that you think are effective and practice these.

Rehearsal Checklist

If you are having trouble rehearsing behaviors check yourself on the following:

- You have not carefully identified the behaviors that you wish to learn.
- You have not identified the contexts specifically enough.
- You are moving too fast, that is, moving on to difficult behaviors or those which induce moderate discomfort before mastering easier ones with which you are fairly comfortable.
- If using covert rehearsal (practicing in your imagination), you may not be imagining the situations clearly enough.
- You may need more help in identifying the behaviors you should practice.
- You could ask a friend to help or devote more attention to watching what other people do who are successful.
- You may not be taking advantage of learning from models.
- Be sure you are offering yourself *positive* feedback.

4

Trying Out New Behaviors: Selecting Assignments

Start with an assignment with which you feel fairly comfortable, which is possible to perform, which you have the skills to carry off successfully and, keeping these considerations in mind, which brings you closest to your objectives. Gradually approaching anxiety-provoking situations and preparing yourself by learning needed skills will make you more confident and help to insure your success.

How to Begin

It may be necessary to start with assignments that seem far removed from your final goal. Let's say your goal is to be able to initiate conversations with unacquainted women in a variety of situations, but you feel too uncomfortable to do this even after you have rehearsed these situations frequently. You could practice starting conversations with male acquaintances, then female acquaintances, and finally with women you don't know. Perhaps your goal is to engage in more extended contacts with men and women, but you have trouble keeping a conversation interesting for ten minutes. Your first step could be to practice maintaining conversations for shorter periods, for example, for only five minutes. This goal may seem a long way from the goal you eventually wish to achieve, but progressing in a gradual, step-by-step manner will increase the likelihood of ultimate success.

Be careful not to overburden yourself with too many assignments. You can combine assignments. You may, for example, want to try out a new way of initiating conversations as well as a new way of increasing your participation in a conversation. You could carry these out within the same exchanges. Perhaps you wish to increase contacts with both strangers and acquaintances. A possible first assignment would be to double the number of initiations you make during the next week. Prior to doing this you may wish to read Chapter 8 on initiating conversations.

If there are certain topics you are afraid to handle, you should not introduce these first, but decide beforehand on "safe" ones to bring up. Watson and Tharp presented an example of a woman who wanted to meet more men but felt uncomfortable when discussing controversial topics but comfortable in talking about topics such as the weather. At first she could only introduce topics of conversation she felt comfortable talking about. As her comfort increased, she could then select other topics to introduce which made her just slightly uncomfortable and so on, until she felt free to engage in conversations in which highly controversial content was discussed.

If you are overly sensitive to being rebuffed, you should first prepare yourself with some coping skills to deal with this (see Chapter 14).

Keeping Records

You may find it useful to keep a record of completed assignments so you will know when to progress to more advanced ones. A form is provided for this in Appendix G. This allows notation of the date, the assignment number, a description of the assignment, whether you carried it out and the date it was completed. Be as specific as possible. Include any limits you place upon your behavior, such as not bringing up certain topics as well as any special requirements like the length of a conversation.

Each person might start at a somewhat different point. Use the information you collected during assessment to help you take a careful look at your own behavior so you can select an appropriate beginning point. Sample assignments are offered at the end of each chapter where relevant.

Given that you change your behavior gradually, there should be a number of intermediate steps by which to carry out your assignments. The term "intermediate steps" refers to behaviors that lie between where you start your program and your final objectives. These can be written down in order of increasing difficulty so that you will have an "agenda" available. You may start with increasing the number of times you initiate brief conversations (more than a greeting) with strangers or acquaintances. After you successfully accomplish this, you may initiate longer interactions, say those which last for five mintes. After successfully maintaining conversations which are five minutes long, try to arrange for the continuation of a meeting over a beer or cup of coffee. The next step is to arrange for a later meeting. You should not go on to a more difficult or complex assignment until you have successfully carried out less difficult ones. In addition to increasing the number and duration of interactions which you initiate, you may also wish to increase their enjoyability, to arrange for future meetings, and to initiate contacts with different types of people.

The exact size of the steps involved—for example, how many contacts to initiate, how long the interactions will last—will vary from person to person. The information from your summary sheet, feedback from rehearsing, and notations on the behavior assignment sheets will guide you in the selection of assignments. A sample list of graduated assignments is shown below.

During the next week, initiate two brief conversations (more than a greeting) with a stranger and two with acquaintances.

During the next week, initiate and maintain two longer conversations (ten minutes) with strangers plus two longer ones with acquaintances.

During the next week arrange for the continuation of an interaction with a stranger or an acquaintance (must last at least 20 minutes).

During the next week arrange for a later meeting (at least one hour) with either an acquaintance or a stranger whom you have just met.

During the next week initiate an extended interaction (at least two hours) with a stranger and/or acquaintance.

As you can see from the list above some assignments involve doing more of the same, such as spending more time talking, initiating more conversations, whereas others involve different behaviors, for example, arranging future meetings and initiating conversations. Keep in mind that an important criteria for selecting harder assignments is whether you are successful with easier ones. If you select the assignment of arranging for future contacts and you ask five people and they all turn you down, then you should stop and examine your behavior. Each person should progress at his/her own pace. If in doubt as to whether you should proceed or not, it is better to overlearn than to risk premature failure. On the other hand, you may find that you underestimated your skills and comfort levels and that you can move faster than you had projected.

How To Increase Your Success

Initiating contacts, trying to arrange for future meetings, and so forth always entail the risk of being turned down. A helpful agreement to have with yourself is that you will keep on trying until you are successful. Let's say your assignment is to start a conversation with a stranger, find out her/his name and go have a cup of coffee. Your obligation to yourself could be to continue to try until you succeed. If you think the assignment is too difficult for you because it causes too much discomfort or requires skills that you lack, then the assignment you selected is premature, and you select one that is easier. Failure with an assignment may mean that you have neglected to learn and practice some behaviors that are crucial for its success. For example, if you wish to increase the frequency with which you set up future meetings over the phone, perhaps you have not prepared for the phone conversation by previously selecting potential places to go. Another reason for failure may be that you have practiced a behavior in the wrong situation. If you wish to meet more women (to date) and only approach one when she is deeply engrossed in talking to another man, then no matter how refined your speaking skills, you are not likely to get very far because you have selected the wrong time to approach her.

Where relevant, checklists are included at the end of chapters which can be used to identify what you may need to learn and practice to increase your success. For any assignment you select, identify the general areas of skill involved, and go over them before trying the assignment. Your skills and comfort level can be increased by practicing behaviors before attempting an assignment. Use the techniques discussed in the previous chapter. You should not try an assignment unless you feel fairly comfortable about trying it out, have practiced it, and believe that you have a high probability of success. If you complete an assignment with great ease, then you probably have selected one that was too easy and should select a more demanding one. Try to note what you did that was related to your success so these skills will be readily at hand on future occasions. As soon as you complete one assignment successfully a few times and feel comfortable with this, go on to the next one. Be sure to reinforce yourself for each attempt (see Chapter 5). If you complete an assignment but still feel uncomfortable doing it, continue to practice it until your comfort increases before progressing on to a more difficult one. In this way, the probability of success will remain high and your discomfort low as you learn new skills and go on to more difficult tasks. Remember, we learn by doing. The more practice you arrange, the easier it will be to start a conversation or express disagreement.

There are two ways you can entice yourself to carry out an assignment that you don't feel like doing. You can make the assignment easier by requiring a lower skill level or arranging for a higher comfort level. If you can't get yourself to maintain a conversation for 30 minutes, then you might reduce your goal to 15 minutes, or, if you feel uncomfortable in a bar, you might want to choose another situation in which to practice your assignment or, you can make it easier by offering yourself a reward for engaging in the behavior. A mild amount of discomfort is to be expected when trying out new behaviors or old behaviors in new situations. Some of what you may label as discomfort may result from positive anticipation of an interesting encounter. You may mislabel the latter as discomfort when your arousal is more correctly interpreted as "excitement."

Giving Yourself Incentives

Getting yourself to do things you don't feel like doing is usually what people mean by "exercising willpower." As Watson and Tharp point out, a lack of willpower can be viewed as a failure to select appropriate assignments or to arrange for rewards for their accomplishment. Offering yourself incentives may be important in the early stages of your program before the natural reinforcing consequences of more enjoyable and frequent social contacts have a chance to take effect (see Chapter 5).

Assignment Checklist

If you are having problems consider the following:

- You may be going too fast. There may be needed skills you do not possess. Or the assignment may cause too much discomfort. You may need to spend more time developing coping skills for anxiety management (see Chapter 14).
- Perhaps you are trying to do too much at once. Maybe you are trying to increase how often you smile, look at others, ask others for their opinion, in addition to other things, and you become confused and distracted during your encounters.
- Are you offering yourself praise for carrying out assignments? You may offer yourself an incentive for trying assignments.
- Perhaps you are not selecting well-defined tasks to accomplish. You may have to spend more time trying to identify what to do differently.
- You may be going too slow. You may be selecting assignments that are too easy. If so, you should choose more demanding ones.
- You may not have selected an appropriate situation to perform the assignment.

5

Self-reinforcement

All of us gain motivation to accomplish an objective if we reward our-selves for doing it. Self-reinforcement consists of offering yourself some positive consequence after you engage in a behavior that you wish to strengthen or increase or refrain from a behavior that you wish to decrease. Developing and using self-reinforcement is emphasized here for several reasons. First, positive social consequences for new behaviors may be somewhat delayed until skills are relatively well established. You may have to go through many small steps before your efforts are rewarded by an enjoyable interaction. Self-reinforcement can help to bridge this gap. Behaviors maintained by self-reinforcement can persist in spite of a low rate of positive feedback from others. You can reinforce yourself for small accomplishments regardless of whether they are noticed by others. This will make it easier to persevere in the initial stages of your program.

In addition, self-reinforcement can help you to maintain your new skills over time. Such reinforcement can be an enduring source of positive feedback while being relatively independent of the evaluative responses of others. Self-reinforcement is a very important aspect of your efforts to change your social behavior and to maintain your new skills. Positive consequences that you can offer yourself include things you say to yourself, and things you allow yourself to do. The first category includes praising or complimenting yourself openly. The second involves activities or items you enjoy which you can offer yourself only after you do something effectively. For example, if you promise yourself to start a conversation with the new person at work today, you can buy yourself a steak for dinner tonight (or call a friend, read a favorite novel for one hour, or play tennis).

Developing Self-Praise

Self-praise is generally the final step in a three-stage process. The first step involves self-observation, that is, deliberately watching your own behavior so that you know when you have done something well. The second step is self-evaluation or judging whether or not your behavior meets your expectations and, if so, to what degree. And finally, self-reinforcement is gained if you judge your behavior adequate or above what you expected. In practice, these three components become an integrated process: you observe your behavior, determine its adequacy and praise yourself accordingly.

If you are not in the habit of complimenting yourself, you are strongly encouraged to give yourself praise when you deserve it. A "counter" on which points can be recorded is helpful in the development of self-reinforcement. The counter performs two functions. You can use it to keep track of the number of compliments you give yourself during the day and it is a cue or signal that reminds you to praise yourself for your successes. A golf counter that is worn like a watch can be used; it is relatively small, is portable, and it can be placed in a pocket or purse. It can be purchased at department, sports, or discount stores.

This is not to suggest you click your counter while engaged in conversation. Not only could this severely hamper conversation, but also will become rather annoying. Just try to remember how many compliments you give yourself and count it on your counter after contact has ended—but don't wait too long or you may not remember accurately.

If you decide to use a counting device, you should employ the following procedure. After you engage in a behavior you wish to strengthen, for example, initiating a conversation with a stranger, give yourself a compliment and a certain number of points that indicate your evaluation of your behavior. Be sure that your compliment is a genuine one and not a "sugar-coated" self-criticism. Some examples of positive self-evaluative statements are show below. Each person may differ as to what particular statements are meaningful to use. You should therefore determine your own unique list of such statements:

"I really did a good job."

"(your name), you did it!"

"I gave a very thorough argument."

"Now, that took a lot of courage."

"Great!"

"A very good response . . ."

Examples of "sugar-coated" criticisms or pseudo-self-praise might include:

"Well, that wasn't too great, but I guess it will do."

"I did it but I'm afraid I sounded dumb."

"I did OK, but I could have done better."

"That wasn't too bad . . ."

When learning how to make social contacts it is important to praise every step toward your final objectives, regardless of how small. It is tempting to be overly self-critical at the beginning of a change program because successes may seem small. You should not allow self-criticism to contaminate your self-praising efforts. Instead, all forms of self-criticism should be boycotted when you are concentrating on self-praise and giving yourself points. If you find yourself beginning to indulge in criticism, stop yourself immediately by saying, for example, "OK, now just *stop* it. I did fine and I'm *not* going to run myself down!" or "Remember the rule, no self-criticism."

The number of points you "award" yourself after you praise your efforts depend on your evaluation of your behavior. Give yourself at least one point for every attempt to improve your social contacts regardless of how clumsy or anxiety-provoking they may seem at first. Give yourself a compliment and one point for a minimum performance and two points for an exceptional one. In this way every attempt is rewarded, some attempts more than others. *Never* subtract points or criticize yourself for a performance you consider to be inferior. Give yourself at least one point for trying and concentrate on what you can learn from your experience. You should concentrate on constructive thoughts, saying, "Well, at least I tried and I learned something." Then try to identify a more effective response.

Keeping a record of the total number of points you award yourself each day will be a reminder to use self-praise and will also let you know whether your self-reinforcement is increasing or decreasing. You could keep track of points awarded in the space on the right edge of Checklist A.

To get in the habit of praising yourself and awarding yourself points, practice these behaviors in private first before trying them out in real situations. Also practice offering yourself self-praise and points when rehearsing other behaviors. Verbalize your self-compliment *outloud* at first and then administer points. For example, when you rehearse different ways of initiating a conversation you could praise yourself outloud and give yourself points after each attempt. Many people are taught to be modest and humble even when they do well. Complimenting yourself outloud can help reduce the reluctance you may have about self-praise. After you practice overt self-compliments about ten times or so, then allow your self-praise to become covert or subvocal while you continue to give yourself points on your counter.

When the inner response of self-praise is well established, the counter can be used less frequently, for example, every other day, then once a week; however, you may still use the counter occasionally to reinforce yourself in difficult situations or if your rate of positive evaluative statements starts to decrease.

Arranging Rewards

Another form of self-reinforcement is arranging positive rewards for engaging in some desirable behavior. There are several criteria that should be considered when developing workable rewards. The first is remembering to progress in small steps. Workable contingencies, or giving yourself rewards, are dependent on the accomplishment of your goal; allow for the attainment of *small* successes in order to gain positive consequences. For example, if disagreeing is difficult for you, then you might be more likely to get yourself to disagree once with an acquaintance at first than fifteen times with strangers, no matter how magnificent the reward is for doing so. Another element in setting up workable contingencies has to do with the *timing* of the reward you arange for yourself. Rewards that occur *immediately* after behavior tend to have more reinforcement potential than those which are delayed. A phone call to a friend after work would probably be more of an incentive to initiate a conversation with a new employee than would the same call five days later. Arrange for positive consequences that you can indulge in as soon as possible after you fulfill your assignment. You may decide to use points on your counter to determine what kind of reward to give yourself. You could give yourself a point each time you accomplish something and then reward yourself at the end of the day according to the number of points earned. If you wish to increase the number of times you express opinions, you record each response on your counter. Then allow yourself a choice of rewards from a reinforcement "menu" depending on the number of points earned. Establish an agreement with yourself that if you earn from one to five points you can choose from among several possible consequences (reading a magazine when eating dinner, listening to a favorite record for 15 minutes); if you earn between six and ten points, then you can choose from slightly more desirable activities; and if you earn 11 to 15 points, you can go to a movie or go shopping. A menu allows you to reinforce yourself for a minimal performance in addition to offering special bonuses for an exceptional performance.

In arranging contingencies, specify exactly what behavior is involved and precisely what the reinforcer will be. For instance, if you want to increase conversations with strangers, it would be necessary to determine the length of such conversations required to earn a reward. If you decide that one brief conversation with a stranger is worth one long distance phone call, then you would have to decide on how long a "brief" conversation is as well as how long the call will last. After you decide how much behavior is required, then you must determine how much of the reinforcer you can sample. Will you allow yourself a five-minute, 10-minute, or 30-minute long distance call? The exchange should be a fair one involving a reasonable amount of reinforcer in exchange for the behavior. In the above example, you might decide that a 10-minute long distance call is equivalent to a brief conversation. (Sample contingencies are listed at the end of this chapter.)

You may have some difficulty at first in deciding on positive consequences. Perhaps your financial situation will not allow for steak dinners, long distance phone calls or new clothes as reinforcers. There are two ways around this problem. You could use points as immediate reinforcers and promise yourself a reward at a later date. You could give each point a monetary value and save for a desired item or an evening out. For instance, every point you earn could be considered a dime or a quarter toward a larger monetary goal. You could even have a container where you deposit your earned coins at the end of each day. Seeing the number of coins accumulating could help bridge the delay between the behavior and the eventual reward.

Another way to avoid using expensive items or activities as reinforcers is to select everyday pleasant events as immediate positive consequences for successes. There are many events that occur in our everyday lives that can be used as effective reinforcers. Either things, people or activities can function as reinforcers. Things are tangible items such as a candy bar, a new pair of shoes, or a science fiction book. People reinforcers involve having coffee with a good friend or telephoning your sister. Activities can mean going somewhere, taking a walk, watching TV, playing chess and so on. To help you recognize a number of possible reinforcers that are available to you, list three under each category below. This list will be the beginning of a catalog of potential reinforcers that you can use as incentives to make your change efforts easier. As you discover new ones, add them to the list. We each have our own reinforcement "profile." What may be pleasant to someone else, may not be important to you. Give some thought to what you like to do, what you would like to have, what you do in your spare time, and so on. With this information, design contingencies that will help you reach your objectives. The items listed on the Activity Inventory (Appendix K) may help you decide what rewards might appeal to you.

Potential Reinforcers

Things	People	Activities
1.	1.	1.
2.	2.	2.
3.	3.	3.

Even though you arrange a positive consequence for yourself, it may not always be easy to get yourself to carry out an assignment because it involves putting off a pleasurable event until you have completed your goal. The best way to make it easier is to make the assignment as much fun as possible, and when you complete the assignment, offer yourself something you ordinarily would not give yourself.

Sample Contingencies

If I initiate one brief conversation with a stranger today, then I can listen to one side of my new album tonight.

If I maintain a conversation with a stranger for more than 15 minutes, then I can make a 10-minute long distance phone call.

If I arrange for a future meeting with a new acquaintance (out to coffee, out to lunch), then I can buy a recent bestseller.

If I go to a coffeehouse by myself on a week night and stay for one drink, then I can have a dish of chocolate ice cream when I get home.

If I go to the coffeehouse by myself on a Friday night and stay for 30 minutes and initiate one conversation, then I can invite a friend to go bicycling on Saturday afternoon.

If I can maintain an enjoyable conversation with a new acquaintance for an extended period of time (over one hour), then I can buy two tickets for the baseball game.

If I can double the number of opinions I give during daily conversations, then I can have $2 extra spending money for myself for each day that I accomplish this goal.

Checklist

If you are having trouble increasing self-reinforcement scan the following list:

Self-Praise

• You may not really know whether the frequency of your positive self-statements is increasing or decreasing since you are not counting how often you offer self-praise.

- Perhaps you have not identified positive self-statements that are specific and believable to you.
- You may need to practice offering yourself positive self-statements before trying to increase these in actual situations.
- You may have to identify a variety of positive self-statements, otherwise those you employ may become "old hat" and not meaningful.
- You may be setting your expectations too high and thus not providing an oportunity to offer many positive self-statements. Remember to select approximations to your final objectives which you can readily accomplish. Frequent reinforcement is important in altering behavior.
- You may have to set up a special contingency to increase positive self-statements. For example, you may agree that, "If I reinforce myself at least five times today I can purchase one of my favorite magazines."
- Perhaps you are forgetting to offer yourself positive statements immediately after desirable conduct. You may have to employ a cue at first to remind you to do this.

Arranging Contingencies

- Perhaps you are not enforcing the contingency.
- You may expect too much behavior for too little reinforcement.
- Promised positive events may be too delayed. You may have to arrange some form of immediate reinforcement if you are working toward a long-term goal, such as points on a counter.

6

Finding Out What Is Happening

Evaluating your progress can be very helpful. It enables you to select appropriate assignments and lets you know whether your efforts are bearing results. If you are now successful in maintaining five-minute conversations and have demonstrated your ability a number of times, this fact informs you that you are now ready to set another goal, for example, ten-minute conversations. Attempting to change behavior without recognizing how far you have realistically progressed can be discouraging or falsely heartening. You may be making progress when you don't think you are, or, conversely, you may think that things are changing when in fact nothing has happened. Counting the number of times you engage in a behavior, combined with charting your progress on a graph, may be helpful.

In order to evaluate your progress, you must monitor (keep track of) your behavior, thoughts or feelings. This section will offer guidelines for how to monitor yourself as well as show you how to use graphs to display your progress over time. Remember that you must be able to specifically identify a behavior, thought or feeling you are trying to record and change. You should be certain when the behavior occurs or does not occur so that you can keep track of it easily and accurately and assess whether it is changing. Trying to count vaguely defined states such as "being a good conversationalist" is difficult because what constitutes a "good conversationalist" is not specified. In contrast, such behaviors as introducing new topics of conversation and offering opinion statements are specific and can be observed and counted.

When You Should Monitor Your Behavior

Monitoring behavior before you try to change it provides a baseline against which you can compare what happens after you change efforts. You should keep track of the behavior you want to change both before as well as after you try to change it. When you reach your final goals and your behavior has remained stable for a week or two, you can reduce the consistency with which you keep track of your behavior. Let's say your goal is to initiate two conversations per day and that you have maintained this for two weeks. Thereafter you could just record your behavior every other day, then every third day, every other week, and so forth. You should periodically check to see whether your behavior has been maintained or whether there has been some slippage. If you are moving on to an intermediate assignment, let's say to initiate four conversations a day, you would continue monitoring your behavior to determine when you reach this next objective.

Selecting a Way to Record

There are many different ways you can keep track of a behavior, thought or feeling. It is important that you select a recording procedure which is accurate as well as easy for you to carry out.

Continuous Recording

You could count how often a behavior occurred during all your interactions or just during a sample of these. During assessment, for example, you were encouraged to keep a frequency count of the number of conversations you initiated with people you wished to see more often. With low frequency behaviors, recording a behavior every time it occurs may not be difficult and you may gather a total frequency count and determine the daily frequency of a behavior. You can keep track by marking a line on a small 3" x 5" card each time it occurs on a chart such as shown.

Day	Shared information about myself
Mon	
Tue	
Wed	
Thur	
Fri	
Sat	
Sun	

With behaviors that occur more often, it may be too bothersome to gather a total weekly count, and you may decide to record your behavior only during selected time periods. You will first have to select the time period when you will monitor your behavior. Let us say that you eat dinner at a cafeteria every night and usually sit with someone and talk. Record the number of opinion statements you make during this time. You should also note the duration of the exchanges because if these differ from day to day, you will have to determine the *rate* of your behavior in order to obtain a fair estimate. Let's say you started talking at 5:30 and finished the conversation at 6:00, and made five opinion statements during this time. You can determine your rate of behavior by dividing the number of behaviors by the number of minutes. In this case your rate of behavior would be .16 per minute (30 / 5 = .16).

One advantage of using rate as a measure is that it allows you to compare your behavior even though different time periods were used. Perhaps on Monday you only record your behavior for a half-hour whereas on Tuesday you observe your behavior in three different conversations which lasted a total of two hours. Because rate involves a common indicator (number per minute or per hour), these different time periods can easily be compared. However, different time periods should be grouped together only if they represent equivalent situations. If you were trying to increase the frequency with which you ask other people for their opinion and it is much easier for you to ask men than women, you should separately compare these two situations in assessing your progress. Another advantage of rate as a measure of change is that it enables you to compare what is happening with very different behaviors. You may not only wish to increase the number of elaborated opinion statements you offer but also to increase the number of times you ask others for their opinion. Use of rate as a measure would allow the comparison of what is happening with these two behaviors.

If you record your behavior during several different periods in any one day and wish to obtain the rate for that day, add up the total number of hours or minutes (depending on whether you are interested in rate per minute or rate per hour) and the total number of behaviors. By dividing the amount of time into the number of behaviors, you can arrive at the rate for that day.

Unless you record for the same time period each day or take a total frequency count, you will have to convert your information to rate to obtain an accurate estimate. A recording form that can be used to gather either a total frequency count or to count behavior only during selected times is included in Appendix H. This form allows room to note the date, the time you start and stop recording, the total time, the number of behaviors noted and the daily rate. Recording of information should be done as soon as possible following an interaction.

Time Samples

Another type of recording procedure which may be useful involves observing your behavior at certain times to see whether you are engaging or did engage in a particular behavior. Let us say that you are trying to increase the frequency with which you compliment others during conversations. Note whether you complimented the other person during each exchange. After each conversation, try to recall whether you offered a specific compliment. A recording form for this type of monitoring appears in Appendix I. Indicate a "yes" in the space provided on this form if you offered one or more compliments during an exchange. At the end of each day, determine the percentage of interactions which were more than just a greeting in which you offered a compliment. If you engaged in eight conversations in one day and only offered compliments during two, then your success rate would be 25 percent (8 / 2 = .25). That is, in 25 percent of your conversations you achieved your goal of complimenting the person at least once.

Select a specific number of times to check on your behavior per day and see if the behavior is occurring at these times. This procedure is useful if a behavior, thought or feeling can occur frequently during a day. For example, note five times per day when you are relaxed during your conversations. Notations can be made on the form in Appendix I. A daily percentage is determined by dividing the number of times you checked on your behavior into the number of times your were engaging in the behavior, experiencing the feeling, or thinking a given thought.

Keep in mind that you must specify what it is that you want to observe; otherwise, you may change your criterion as to whether a behavior occurred or not and, if so, you will not be able to accurately assess whether your behavior is changing.

Recording forms should be conveniently located, for example, in a pocket or purse so they are realily available. In order to fit more easily they can be on index-sized cards. A counter can also be kept in a pocket or purse.

Graphing Your Behavior

It is often helpful to chart information about behavior so that you can visually see how your behavior is changing or more readily compare one behavior with another. Perhaps you wish to compare the number of exchanges per week you initiate with men with the number you initiate with women. You could chart the weekly frequency of initiations separately for men and for women on the same graph. Some time measure, weeks or days, is noted at the bottom of the chart and some measure of behavior at the left. If you wish to chart the weekly number of times you initiate conversations, indicate on the chart the point corresponding to the number of times you initiate a conversation for each week. These data points are connected with lines so you can more readily see the trends in your behavior.

Be sure to note what measure you are using to the left of the graph as well as the time interval at the bottom of the graph. Arrange your chart so that changes can be seen easily. Don't confine all the data to a small part of the graph. Spread it out so you can see what is happening. If there is a day or week during which the behavior you are keeping track of could not occur, for instance, if you were ill, this can be indicated by placing a circle around the date(s) on the horizontal axis. This will let you know that there was no opportunity for the behavior to occur at these times. A blank chart is provided in Appendix J.

You will obtain useful feedback if you chart your progress on a weekly basis. You can easily transfer the information from your daily records to your chart at the end of the week. You could, of course, chart on a daily basis if you like. Keep your chart where it will have the most impact on your behavior. If you want immediate access to it at home, you could post it on a wall. Feedback itself can motivate change in your behavior.

Evaluation Checklist

If you are having trouble evaluating your progress:

- You may not have specified the behavior, thought, and/or feeling that you want to keep track of.

- You may have selected a recording procedure that is too difficult. You may be trying to count too many things or otherwise using a procedure that is too complicated or time consuming. If so, select an easier one.

- You may have selected a recording procedure which interferes with your social exchanges.

- You may forget to record your behavior. You should arrange some cue that will serve as a reminder. The cue can be anything as long as it does not interfere with your social exchanges and reminds you to record, such as wearing a counter, or having an index card in your pocket.

- You may think that you know what is going on without bothering to compare the rate of some behavior, thought, or feeling before and after you try to change it and you may be correct. However, you may be incorrect and so will not know what is happening. If you have doubts, you could compromise by giving recording a try to see whether the feedback provided is helpful to you.

- You may plot your data on a very small graph so that even considerable progress looks miniscule.

7

Where To Go To Meet People

It is possible that one big reason you do not have more social contacts is that you do not take advantage of the situations you already find yourself in, such as work or school. You may not go to the places where the chances of meeting new people are possible. You may have the mistaken idea that there are no places to meet people you like or that such places are difficult to find. You must learn to look at your environment to determine where you can meet people and where your own interests will be stimulated. This chapter will show you how to take advantage of the opportunities that surround you.

How to Locate Promising Places

A promising place to meet people should satisfy two criteria: people who you would like to meet will be there, and the situation offers some activity, such as hiking or playing chess, which you enjoy. Thus, one way to select places to meet others is to take an inventory of your own interests. What types of activities do you like? An Activity Inventory has been developed to enable you to list your interests as well as to note how often, in the past month, you have participated in each (see Appendix K). This inventory will allow you to see how often you participate in activities which you enjoy and which also might enable you to meet people. All activities listed offer the possibility of meeting others. Scan the inventory and select two activities that are particularly appealing to you as well as possible to engage in. For example, if you selected hiking, are hiking clubs available in your area and do they provide an opportunity to meet people you would like? If you wish to meet more men and find that the hiking club in your area consists of 75 percent women, then you would not select this activity. To determine suitable activities, you can start by gathering information via phone calls. Check your main library, the Y.W.C.A., other community centers. Seek out bulletin boards that might contain posters describing activities, look through catalogues and newspapers, and so forth. You may want to insure continual, updated information on activities by subscribing to the local newspaper, or requesting to be put on the mailing lists for adult education classes or for program information from neighborhood community centers. Through your efforts you may discover other activities which interest you. You will also have to find out *when* the activities occur to make sure they fit into your schedule. Other important points of information include requirements for joining, fees involved and special equipment needed.

For the two activities that you select, find out which of the various groups in your area engage in the activity and how to contact them. You should select the one that is best suited for your purposes. For each group, find out whether the people you would like to meet participate, and to what extent. You might say when you call: "I'd like to find out some information about your hiking club. About how many people usually go along on the hikes? (Wait for an answer.) "Are there an equal number of men and women who participate?" If a reasonable proportion of individuals you wish to meet participate, then you can find out when, where, and how often they meet, as well as requirements for joining. The information you obtain will automatically rule out some possibilities. The hiking club may only be for experienced climbers and you may be a novice. Beginning hiking clubs may only be offered during a certain time of the year, or the scuba diving club may require a fee which is beyond your means, or only men might participate and you may wish to meet more women. For activities that seem to be a possibility now or in the future, note them in some systematic way so that the information is readily available. You could use an index card for each one on which you record the activity, name of the group, their phone number, meeting times, and so forth. This will provide you with a file of interesting things to do in your own area. The card below illustrates information that should be placed on each card.

---

activity: group hiking

1. Sierra Club:

                                    a. address: _____

meeting times: _____   b. phone number: _____

_____   c. requirements: _____

place of meetings: _____

_____   d. fee: _____

Date of first meeting: _____

Can I satisfy requirements of the group: Yes ___ No ___

Who could I meet through participation in this group?

_____

Taking Advantage of Everyday Activities

Many time you can meet others simply in the course of everyday activities: going to the laundry, library or supermarket. Keep in mind that these situations often provide an opportunity to meet others. They also provide a ready topic for conversation—the situation in which you are both present. For example, if you are in a bookstore, you could say, "Excuse me. I was wondering if you could recommend a good novel?"

Situations that provide opportunities for meeting others could be sought out more frequently. Rather than going to the library once a month, you might go once a week. If you would like to meet people who are doctors or potential doctors, some cities have physicians' libraries in addition to medical school libraries. It would, of course, be more enjoyable to decide upon something you wanted to find out at the library so that you will be following a personal interest. This interest might also provide a topic for conversation. Other places that may provide opportunities to meet others include elevators, buses, trains and lunch counters.

Taking Advantage of Special Events

No matter how small the town or city, there are special events that occur at different times of the year and provide opportunities for meeting others, often in an atmosphere of festivity, such as fairs, parades and shows. There may also be opportunities to help plan the event. This often involves working with a group of people who you can get to know. Get in the habit of reading bulletin boards and newspapers on a weekly basis to find out what special events are coming up that might provide an opportunity for fun, interesting activities, and meeting others.

Criteria for Selecting Places

Two important criteria for selecting places to go have already been mentioned—whether people will be present who you would like to meet and whether the activity interests you. Other criteria allow you to select places in keeping with your skill and comfort levels. For example, situations differ in terms of the amount of pressure for social contacts. Going to a movie involves much less pressure than a party. Some situations also differ in terms of pressure to stay for a given period of time. In some cases, the participants are free to come and go as they wish, whereas others, such as a class, require you to remain for a certain length of time. Contexts also differ in terms of the opportunities for initiating conversations as well as the degree to which they provide ready topics of conversation. Any situation that is built around an activity has a built-in topic for conversation. Situations also differ in terms of how comfortable you will feel when in them and the likelihood that people will start conversations with you. Thus, when scanning environments to decide which to sample the checklist below can be used as a guide.

Situations:	Great Deal	Moderate	Little
Degree of pressure for social interaction.			
Degree of pressure to stay for a period of time.			
Opportunities for making contacts you would like.			
Degree to which situation provides topics of conversation.			
How comfortable you are.			
How much you like the activity involved.			
Opportunities for initiating conversations.			

Characteristics of a situation may be related. For instance, the degree of comfort you feel may be related to the degree of pressure for interaction. Select situations in which you are fairly comfortable, which have a high probability for making contacts, and which provide ready topics for conversation. You can then move on to more difficult situations as you acquire skill and self-assurance.

Forming a Beginning List of Places

The table below is provided to help you list activities that satisfy the criteria previously discussed for selection of places to meet people. In column I, list the two activities you selected from the Activity Inventory as well as everyday ones. In column II, note places where you can practice social behaviors even though they might not provide opportunities for meeting individuals with whom you would like to have more contacts. For purposes of practice, one of the criteria for selecting

I Places to meet others	II Places for practice only
1.	1.
2.	2.
3.	3.
4.	4.
5.	5.
6.	6.

places (meeting people with whom you wish to have more contacts) can be disregarded. For example, if initiating contacts with strange males is too fearful for you, you could frequent places where you can practice initiating conversations with men you already know. Although your final goal may be to increase contacts with unacquainted males and seek out various places where such men might be present, a first step might be to place yourself in situations where you can practice behaviors with "safe" males.

You can increase opportunities for meeting people by taking a more active role in initiating social contacts. You should consider any situation a potential one for initiating conversations. The laundry is not just a place to wash your clothes; it can also provide a chance to have enjoyable social contacts and to practice your new skills on someone you might wish to see on other occasions. You are encouraged to use the Situation Summary form located in Appendix B to keep track of the situations in which you meet people. This will provide feedback as to how many you are sampling and who you meet in each.

Sample Assignments

If you do not go many places to meet others, then selecting new places to visit, and initiating conversations while there, should be part of your assignments. You could combine these assignments with others which involve the performance of behaviors such as initiating conversations.

Go to a familiar neighborhood bookstore on a week night and stay for 15 minutes.

Go to an unfamiliar bookstore on a Friday night and stay for 30 minutes.

Do your laundry at a different laundromat in a new neighborhood. Be sure to go alone.

Go to a free Sunday afternoon concert alone and stay for at least 30 minutes.

Attend an art show on a Saturday afternoon by yourself. Take time to see the entire exhibit.

Go to a travel lecture and slide show on a weekday night by yourself. Stay for the entire presentation and then linger afterwards for 10 minutes.

Join a group of people for a Sunday afternoon bicycle trip. Go with a friend or acquaintance and arrive 15 minutes before departure time so you can get acquainted with the others in the group.

Go to a folk dancing place on a week night by yourself. Stay for at least 30 minutes, have a drink, and watch the others dance.

Go again to the folk dancing club alone, but this time go on a Friday night and take the dance lesson.

Join a hiking club for a four-hour Saturday afternoon hike which involves bringing a sack lunch.

With the same hiking group, attend an all-day hike on another Saturday that involves dinner around the campfire.

Go to a coffeehouse with a friend or by yourself on a week night and stay for thirty minutes.

Attend a public hearing of a political issue by yourself on a Wednesday evening. Stay after the meeting for 10 minutes to engage in casual discussion.

Go to a chess club meeting and watch one game played by others before you leave.

Play two games with two different people at the same chess club.

Attend a co-ed volleyball game at the local community center on a Friday night with a friend. After you observe one game, join in for the second.

Checklist

If you are having difficulty going places to meet people:

- Perhaps you obtained the necessary information on desirable places to go, but avoid going, or "forget," or make excuses. If so, offer yourself an incentive to go and see what it's all about. For example, if you want to take folk dancing lessons, you could reward yourself for just going and seeing the place first, then for staying 15 minutes and watching, and finally for staying and taking a dance lesson.

- You may hesitate to commit yourself to a formal program or series of classes before you know more about the activity. Get more information about the commitment involved before making a decision. If you don't feel comfortable in making a lengthy commitment, choose activities where participation can be sporadic, for example, art shows, spectator sports or weekend bicycling groups.

- If you find few desirable people to initiate conversations with in your everyday activities consider changing your routine. For example, a smaller, unfamiliar market may be more conducive to conversation.

8

Initiating Conversations

This chapter will help you acquire additional skills in initiating conversations. Information is provided on how to make contacts with different people in a variety of situations. Learning a variety of ways to handle yourself will help you to be more comfortable with and in control of the exchanges you have with others. The following topics are discussed: ways of initiating conversations, both appropiate and inappropriate; when to approach others; what to do if the person's response is minimal or negative; and responding to the initiations of others.

How to Begin

Some opening remarks can be used with probable success in a wide variety of situations while others are more likely to be well received only in selected contexts. Those in the former category, although more widely used and generally "safe" in terms of what response follows, can become trite in their delivery and so may reduce your initial impact on others. For example, the general opening remarks of "Have you been waiting long?" or "Are you new here?" are frequently used as opening comments. Yet, these may be interpreted by others as the "same old line." Therefore, even though such remarks are generally acceptable, a degree of personal impact may be sacrificed by not using a more novel or more direct approach which expresses intent, such as "Hello. I'd like to get acquainted; can we talk?"

Opening remarks of a more personal or novel nature, while increasing the likelihood of greater personal impact, also carry the risk of making others uncomfortable or angry. You should start out by learning and practicing the less risky opening remarks. A comparison of the effectiveness of three different types of initiating remarks revealed that requesting permission to enter the other person's space ("Excuse me, do you mind if I talk to you?") was more successful than one which contained an admission of incompetence ("Gee, I have trouble talking to others . . .") or one considered a "line" ("Haven't I seen you somewhere before?").

There are at least eight ways of initiating conversations

- Ask a question or make a comment on the situation or mutual activity that you are *both* involved in.
- Compliment the other person on some aspect of his or her behavior, appearance or some other attribute.
- Make an observation or ask a casual question about what the other person is doing.
- Ask if you may join another person or ask him to join you.
- Ask another person for help, advice, an opinion, information.
- Offer something to someone.
- Share your personal opinion or experience.
- Greet the person and introduce yourself.

Many examples could be listed under each category depending upon the context, person involved and so forth. Those illustrated below will give you an idea of the types of opening remarks that are possible under each. As you go over the list, you may find it helpful to think of an example of your own under each category and to write it down in the spaces provided.

For each type listed, you could make a comment, ask a question, or do both. For example, you could offer an opinion, explain briefly why you feel that way, and then ask the other person what s(he) thinks. These variants entail different degrees of commitment from the listener. For example, if you offer a comment, no response may be required. However, if you ask a question, a direct request is made. Different types of initiating statements also offer varying amounts of information about yourself. If your initiating remark consists of a question, you do not offer much of your own thought, but you do convey that you are interested in what the other person has to say and, in addition, provide him with an opportunity to speak. If you make a comment, offer some reasons why you have said this, and also ask the person for her opinion, then you offer something of yourself in addition to providing an opportunity for her to speak. The information you provide about yourself offers a natural source of questions for the other person. Be sure to wait for an answer if you ask a question. Some people make the mistake of asking one question after another which gives the impression that they are not really interested in what others think because they don't even bother to wait for an answer. Appropriate as well as inappropriate examples are included under each category.

There are a variety of ways that a remark may be inappropriate:

It could be too personal. You may request information that someone does not care to share with you, such as "What's your experience with bisexual feelings?" Or it may imply a commitment that s(he) does not wish to make, such as "We could have a lot of fun together." Or you may disclose information of too personal a nature and so make someone uncomfortable such as, "I just found out I'm impotent."

It could be delivered in a negative way, that is, in a cynical or pessimistic manner. For example, you could initiate a conversation with a complaint about a shared experience, (such as waiting in a long line) in a petulant, whining way which might turn off someone—such as "Everything is fouled up these days." Another type of negative opening implies that others are not interested in talking to you, that is, you put yourself down. For example:

"I don't know if this would interest you, but . . ."
"You're probably busy, but . . ."
"I know this sounds stupid but . . ."

It could be interpreted as a personal criticism. Let's say that you see someone who looks really tired. Rather than saying, "You look awful," you could say, "It looks like you've had a rough day."

It could be sarcastic. Sarcasm should be avoided unless it is humorous and is not at the other person's expense. Double meanings may be taken the wrong way and interpreted as negativism or personal criticism.

It could be phrased as an assumption about the person which s(he) finds distasteful. You could be waiting in line to vote and say to the person in front of you, "I bet you're a Democrat."

It could be a judgmental, or dogmatic statement that allows few alternative replies. A remark such as, "I really hate all this junk, don't you?" offers few alternative replies beyond a "yes" or "no." Also, highly critical remarks may set the stage for an abrupt termination of the conversation or an argument because of the dogmatic attitude expressed.

It could be hostile or confrontative, such as, "What do you think you're looking at," in response to someone gazing at you or, "Do you always go around looking like such a slob?"

Your comment could be inappropriate to the situation, that is it could be out of context. Because of a lack of a common situation or because you have not made it clear where your comment is coming from, others may be very puzzled as to what you are talking about and may find it difficult to know how to respond. For example, during intermission at a concert, it would probably be out of context to go up to a stranger and say, "Did you read about the city council's new ordinance?" or while at a chess club to say, "I hear you oppose freeways." (When in doubt, use situational cues in deciding upon opening remarks, such as, "Are you enjoying the concert?" or "I understand that you're also a beginning chess player" in the related situation.)

Familiarizing yourself with some of these typical blunders may help you avoid them when you initiate conversations.

Starting A Conversation—Initiating Remarks

Ask a question or comment on the situation or mutual activity that you are both involved in.

Situation: Standing in line to see a movie.
"How long have you been waiting?"
   Inappropriate: "You look like you've been waiting for hours." (This could be interpreted as criticism.)
"What have you heard about the movie?"
"We must be early. There aren't many people here yet."
   Inappropriate: "It must be a lousy show. We'll probably be the only ones here." (This is a strong judgmental, pessimistic statement.)
"I've heard so many good things about this movie. The ocean scenes are supposed to be outstanding."
"I'm really cold."

Practice exercise: You are looking at a window display and a stranger is standing beside you. You remark _____

_____

Compliment the other person on some aspect of their behavior, appearance or other attribute. Be specific about the source of your compliment. Sincerity is assumed!

Situation: You are in a laundromat.
"That's beautiful, did you make it?"
"You have a really fine tan. Where did you get it?"
   Inappropriate: "You look nice and healthy. How old are you anyway?"
"That material looks very soft. What kind is it?"
Situation: You attend a lecture at the public library. Only a few people are present. You go up to the speaker afterward, and say:
"I really liked your presentation. Will you be here again?"
"You're so enthusiastic. It's contagious. I feel enthused myself now."

Practice exercise: You see an acquaintance who has just had her hair styled. You say: _____

_____

Make an observation or ask a question about what the other person is doing.

Situation: You are seated next to someone having lunch at a counter.
"Excuse me, what did you order?"
    Inappropriate: "You must be starved the way you're eating." (This might imply a personal criticism.)
Situation: You are seated next to a person on the bus.
"I notice you're reading _____. What do you think of it?"
    Inappropriate: "I see you're reading _____. I thought it was terrible." (Too judgmental. May close off possibility of a reply.)
Situation: You see someone sitting on the grass on a bright sunny day and go over and say:
"You seem to be enjoying yourself."
Situation: You are waiting for a bus and the person standing by you is looking at rental ads. You say:
"I notice you are scanning apartment rentals. Are you looking for a place?"

Practice exercise: While at an art museum, you notice a person looking at one painting for a long time. You go up and say: _____
_____

Ask to join the other person or ask the other person to join you.

Situation: You are sitting alone in a coffee shop (or tavern) and another person is looking around for a place to sit.
"Would you like to sit here?"
"I see that you're alone, too, would you like to join me?"
    Inappropriate: "Are you stepping out on your wife tonight?" (Too personal or sarcastic.)
"Would you like to share a bottle of wine with me?"
"You've been looking over here for some time. Would you like to sit down?"
Situation: You are looking around for a place to sit at a restaurant at lunchtime and go over to a person sitting alone.
"May I join you?" (Pause) "I hesitated because you seemed deep in thought."
"Excuse me. May I sit at this table?" Pause and if you receive an affirmative response then say: "I notice you have some maps there. Are you traveling?"
    Inappropriate: "May I join you?" is OK but then to sit down before you get a reply or in the face of a negative reply is not. If you then went on to say: "You must have terrible sense of direc-

tion to need all those maps." No doubt you would be considered obnoxious.

Practice exercise: During a coffee break at work, go up to a new employee and ask him to join you for lunch that afternoon: _____

Ask the other person for help, advice, an opinion, information.
 Situation: Waiting in line at a restaurant.
 "Do you know what the specialty of the house is?"
  Inappropriate: "Did you hear about that terrible accident last week?" (Out of context.)
 Situation: During intermission at a concert, you go up to a person standing alone.
 "What do you think of the concert?"
  Inappropriate: "You must not like the concert. You look bored to death." (Assumption.)
 Situation: You are out walking.
 "Excuse me. Could you help me find a good bakery?"
 Situation: You are in a large toy shop and say to another customer:
 "I'd like to get your opinion on something." (Pause) "What game do you think a seven-year-old boy would prefer?"
 Situation: The first meeting of a woman's group.
 "Why did you choose this particular discussion group?"
  Inappropriate: "Why in the world would you want to come to this group?" (Personal criticism.)

Practice exercise: You are riding a bicycle and at a signal another cyclist pulls up alongside of you. You want to find out the shortest route to the park. You ask:_____

Offer the other person something.
 Situation: You are seated next to someone on an airplane.
 "Would you like a pillow?"
 "Would you like to read this when I'm done?"
 Situation: Someone is trying to arrange a number of bundles in a shopping basket.
 "You seem to be having trouble, can I help?"
  Inappropriate: "It doesn't look like you know what you're doing. Let me help you." (Personal criticism.)

Practice exercise: You are sitting next to a person on a bus, you open a bag of peanuts and turn to him and say: _____

Share your personal experience, opinions, thoughts, etc.
Situation: You are at a lecture.
"It seems he really had a good point about the future effects of over-population. What do you think?"
Inappropriate: "How could anyone agree with that!" (Dogmatic.)
Situation: A dentist's office.
"I'm feeling nervous. How about you?"
Inappropriate: "You must be nervous." (Assumption.)
Situation: You go over to someone standing alone during a concert intermission.
"The audience really seems to like the program. I've looked forward to hearing this for a long time. I particularly liked . . ."
NOTE: It is a good idea to add a couple of sentences after the initial one. Elaborate on your opening remark. This provides more information concerning what you are talking about and allows a person to sample more of your behavior before replying.

Practice exercise: You are at a concert in the park and are enjoying the music very much. You want to share this with someone, so during the intermission you turn to the person next to you and remark: _____

Greet the person and introduce yourself. In some situations, such as at parties, or if brought together by a mutual friend but not introduced, it is appropriate to greet the person and introduce yourself, for example: "Hi, my name is . . ." The other person will probably then introduce himself or herself.

Additional examples of ways to initiate conversations:

Listed below are examples from a study by Goldsmith and McFall of various reactions to specific situations and the opinions of five "peer judges" concerning their competence. C = the number of judges who rated the response as competent and I = the number who rated it as incompetent.

You are at a bar and see an attractive girl sitting alone at a table. You go over and introduce yourself. She says: "Would you like to sit down?" You sit down and there is a moment of silence. She looks over and smiles at you. You respond with:
"I notice you seem rather lonely." (C = 1; I = 2; 2—no opinion)
"I have the most difficult time in the world picking someone up. I don't know what to say or what to do. Why don't you help me out?" (C = 0; I = 4)
"Can I buy you a drink?" (C = 3; I = 0)
(Smile) (C = 2; I = 0)

"You're very attractive." (C = 2; I = 0)

"You have a pleasant smile." (C = 2; I = 0)

Notice that the first reaction implies a negative quality about the woman and may make her uncomfortable and place her on the defensive. The admission of incompetence in the second response is rated unacceptable although such a response may be followed by a different reaction when used by a woman. Note that the response of offering something received the highest number of competent ratings.

You are seated next to two strangers at a large dinner party. As you sit down to eat, the person on your right looks at you and smiles, but doesn't say anything. You say, "Hello." The person nods, smiles again, and keeps looking at you. You say:

"Is there something wrong?" (C = 1; I = 1)

"Haven't I seen you someplace before?" (C = 0; I = 0)

"How did you come to be invited to this party? Do you know the host?" (C = 3; I = 0)

"Do you have the strange feeling you've seen me before?" (C = 1; I = 0)

"I notice you're smiling." (C = 0; I = 0)

(Look around to see if there is somebody else more receptive.) (C = 0; I = 0)

"I'm Bill Williams. Who are you?" (C = 5; I = 0)

"What is your name? My name is Bill Williams." (C = 4; I = 0)

You are standing in a long checkout line at a department store. A woman standing in front of you has turned around and smiled at you several times. You'd like to chat to pass the time. You say:

"You know, frankly I hate shopping. It's these lines that always discourage me." (C = 2; I = 0)

"Could I help you with the bags?" (C = 1; I = 0)

"This is a real interesting store. Just picked up some snake meat and brass toilet seats." (C = 3; I = 0)

"I think this line would go a lot quicker if we could talk." (C = 0; I = 3)

"I hate standing in line!" (C = 1; I = 1)

"How are you?" (C = 3; I = 0)

"Looks like you have yourself a bundle of groceries." (C = 2; I = 0)

Summary of points to remember when initiating conversations:

Be positive rather than negative   When initiating a conversation, it is better to express your comment in a cheerful way than to sound depressed or bored. A positive approach is likely to put others at ease and stimulate their interest in what you have to say. A positive tone can often be established by merely smiling when you deliver your opening remark, if smiling is appropriate given the context of your message. Thus, *both* your expression as well as your verbal remark can influence how your overtures are received.

Be sure your comment is in context   Make sure your comment relates to a situation or that you share enough of your thoughts so that s(he) knows what you are referring to.

Be as direct as possible   Look directly at the person and voice your intentions. If you would like to sit down next to someone, you will usually accomplish this faster if you simply ask the person. Many people appreciate directness and so you may have a head start in two ways; you will achieve your objective as well as make a good impression. If you employ an indirect opening remark, you may lose out completely. For example, if you ask someone a question such as "Do you have the time?" when in fact you want to sit down and talk to the person, she may just answer your question and turn back to whatever she was involved in. Also make sure you speak loudly and clearly enough to be understood.

Try to be helpful   Attempt to ease the other person's comfort. This may offer a possible appropriate opening remark as well as direct attention away from yourself. Self-consciousness (worrying what others think about you) can detract from your effectiveness in initiating conversations. These thoughts distract you from observing others and so from the possibility of making relevant openings and following up on these.

Take advantage of your sense of humor   People enjoy laughing and it will be a point in your favor if you can make them laugh. The positive part of an opening remark may be the humor with which it is said. That is, you could complain about some aspect of a situation, such as waiting in line, but also add a humorous comment related to this. However, self-consciousness can interfere with spontaneous humorous comments. If humor is not typically a part of your "style" you may want to initiate conversations at first in ways that are comfortable and familiar.

Don't make your opening remarks too long   Allow others to respond to your first comments before making others. A series of statements such as the following should be broken up to allow for replies and comments: "Are you from out of town? I notice that you have a map there. Are you lost? If you are, I can help. I live here . . ."

Ask yourself how you would respond to a remark

Ask open-ended questions   Open-ended questions require more than a yes or no reply. They encourage others to offer more information. For example, you ask, "What did you think of the show?" rather than "Did you like the show?" Open-ended questions may start with "what," "when," "where," "who," "why," and "how."

Note free information that is offered and react to this   Some of the examples mentioned in prior pages involve you in commenting upon something another person is doing. People may also offer additional information in response to a question and you can comment upon or ask questions about this.

Don't try to initiate conversations with people who are deeply engrossed with some other person or activity   A high level of engrossment may mean that the person will not be open to engaging in conversation. Someone intently reading a book and not looking up may not be as likely to respond positively to an overture for conversation as a person who is casually flipping through a magazine and who looks around occasionally. However, one never knows for sure if a person is open to conversation until you try to start one with him or her. Given that you are prepared for a possible minimal or negative reply, we encourage you to try to initiate conversations even in these situations if you are particularly interested in talking to someone. It is easier, when starting to practice initiating exchanges, to select people that appear receptive.

Don't give up too easily   You may have misinterpreted the reserved or cautious response of someone as rejection of your initiating attempts. Often people are cautious about starting conversations with strangers. You can enhance your initial attempts to make contact by sharing appropriate information about yourself or your intentions. You may need to pursue the conversation in spite of a cool response to build up a sense of trust between you and the other person. Of course, if someone continues to appear disinterested or distracted, then you could end the exchange.

Getting rebuffed is not the end of the world.

What to Say if You are Rebuffed

Your comment might have been appropriate but still you may receive a minimal or negative reply. Perhaps the person did not hear you or misinterpreted your comment. Perhaps they are in a sullen mood and would rebuff any overture. Be sure to give yourself a compliment such as, "Well, it was really good that I tried!" for attempting to exert more influence over your social environment and learn what there is to be gained, if anything, from the attempt that failed. Did you violate one of the requisites for initiating conversations? For example, did you deliver your opening remark in a sarcastic or long-winded manner?

How could you be more effective next time? You may find it helpful to jot down possibilities in a log. If the other person seems like a grouch, you could also say to yourself, "Boy what an ill-tempered person he is." Never blame yourself for a failure, or allow a negative thought such as, "Oh my, I never should have tried," or "I feel so embarrassed," or "What a flop I am," to linger. It may be appropriate in the face of a very rude reply to confront the person with their rudeness; however, this may be an advanced behavior which you will have to work up to in terms of comfort. You could say, "You really seem to be in a bad mood today." Being more positive in your self-evaluations will help you persevere in your attempts to initiate social contacts, especially in the face of occasional negative responses from others. Try again unless you receive a reaction that is so negative, there is no question of its intent. The person may welcome a chance to respond in a more positive fashion. At least a second comment from you may clarify your intentions and provide for a more comfortable exit. Some possible reactions to minimal or negative reactions from others are given below:

If you get a minimal response   (response is in parentheses):
Situation: You're standing in a group waiting to be seated in a crowded restaurant:
Ask another question: "Did she say how long the wait might be? (No) Your second question could be combined with offering information about yourself and should be open-ended such as, "I haven't tried this restaurant before. How do you think it compares with other French restaurants in town?"
Elaborate on or repeat your initial remark: "You seem familiar to me. Have we met before?" (No) "Every once in a while I see someone who reminds me of someone else . . ."
Offer a light humorous comment: "Are you new here in Berkeley?" (Uh-huh) "Would you like some tips from a long-time resident?" If minimal responses continue, you could seek out a person who offers more promising possibilities.

If you receive a negative or sarcastic reply.
Situation: You approach someone who is struggling with packages on the street:
Determine if you have offended the person by invading their privacy: "You look like you're having a hard time managing all those bundles." (No, I'm not helpless. I can manage.) "I didn't mean to offend you. I thought you might need some help." Be sure your tone is pleasant and that you sound sincere. Offering a positive reply to a negative comment will often encourage others to be positive in return and may result in an enjoyable encounter.

Situation: You are having a discussion with two people you just met:

Assure the person that you were serious: "That was a good idea." (Oh sure) "I'm quite serious, I . . ." (elaborate)

Situation: Standing in line for a movie:

Respond as if the sarcastic remark was given in humor: "Hmmm, you smell good. Are you wearing anything special?" (Kind of nosey aren't you?) "Well, I guess I do have a good nose on me."

Situation: You are at a craft fair standing by a pottery display:

Ask the person if they are serious or ask for clarification, especially with possible sarcastic comments: "You really look sunburned. Have you been hiking?" (No, I fell asleep under a sunlamp.) "Are you serious?"

Situation: You are seated next to someone sitting alone at lunchtime in a restaurant:

Agree with the person's negative reply: "I notice you're alone too. Would you like to join me?" (Not really. I like being alone.) "I can understand that. I like being alone at times too."

Situation: Someone has dropped a number of papers and is trying to pick them up:

Repeat your initial comment: "You seem to be having trouble, can I help?" (No, I'd rather do it myself.) "OK, but I still think it looks like too much for any one person."

Inititating verbal contact can be made easier by placing yourself in physical proximity to others. By doing this they will be able to hear what you are saying and they can see you. The way can be paved for an opening remark by prior nonverbal contact such as looking at the person, smiling and nodding. Eye contact is a good way to communicate from a distance. Once this has been established, then you can move closer and make verbal contact.

There is some evidence that when seated, men prefer to be approached from the side whereas women prefer to be approached from a face-to-face position, regardless of whether they are approached by a man or a woman. Men reacted negatively when a stranger sat across from them while women reacted negatively when a stranger sat beside them.

Encouraging and Responding to the Initiation of Others

It is important to respond appropriately to the initiation attempts others make. Once you are in a situation where there are people you would like to meet, it is possible that they will attempt to make contact with you. You can facilitate their attempts by appearing open and receptive to initiations and by responding in a positive manner. There are a number of nonverbal behaviors that can enhance your appearing sociable and inviting, including directness of eye contact, smiling frequently, and a relaxed body posture.

Physical attractiveness is an important element in making social contacts, especially in regard to first impressions. Attractiveness means different things to different people, and each of us can enhance the positive attributes that we possess. A variety of characteristics may contribute to one's attractiveness, including complementary clothing (well-fitting, flattering colors and style, appealing color combinations), a flattering hair style cut to enhance your face—not just the latest style; and, the appropriate use of cosmetics to obscure blemishes or enhance features. Neatness and cleanliness also influence how others react to us. Warm bright colors may result in your having a "happier" image which encourages more positive reactions, in contrast to drab or dull tones.

Your appearance should be consistent with the image you wish to portray, the situations in which you try to initiate contacts, and the people you would like to meet. Perhaps you wish to portray a casual image, a person who takes things in their stride, but you dress in an overly formal manner that reflects a different image. Or, perhaps you go to places where the situation requires formal attire and this is not the image you feel comfortable with or wish to cultivate. If you present yourself in a formal way and place yourself in situations that require formal attire, then it is likely that your attempts to portray a casual impression or meet others with this characteristic are reduced.

It is important to *recognize* initiation attempts when they do occur so you can respond positively and encourage further conversation. Recognizing an initiation attempt is not always as easy as it appears. Often, people attempt to start a conversation by using nonverbal or subtle approaches, such as a direct sustained look, or a brief look and a smile, or touching or brushing against you. A question may be asked and offered in a business-like tone, for example, "Do you have the time?" or a half-muttered comment may be made seemingly addressed to no one in particular, but loud enough for you to overhear. For instance, a person next to you may say, "Gee, what a day . . ." To test whether such indirect comments are initiation attempts you could respond and see if the person reciprocates. Sometimes people may ask you global questions such as, "Tell me about yourself" or "What are you interested in?" Such remarks are not recommended for you because others may not know where to begin. A request for clarification such as, "Is there anything in particular you would like to know?" coupled with a suggestion of possible content that is not too personal such as, "I could tell you about what I do," is one possible reaction to such a question.

You may initiate an exchange by writing a note to someone. In fact, in some situations, such as libraries in which quiet has priority, it may be more appropriate to initiate an exchange in such a manner. You could, for example, see someone in a library reading a book and send over a note which says, "Would you like to take a short break for a cup of coffee?" Other ways of setting the stage for speaking to someone include old standbys such as accidentally bumping into a person or throwing a Frisbee in their direction. Hopefully future research will provide more definitive suggestions concerning what types of initiating remarks are most effective in what situations. However, you can be your own "experimenter" by trying out various methods.

Sample Assignments

Experimenting with different ways of initiating contacts increases the frequency and richness of your social exchanges. Assignments you may find valuable to carry out include: trying out new ways to initiate conversations; initiating contacts with a wider range of people; starting conversations in different situations; and initiating more conversations.

While at work, initiate a conversation with a co-worker about a mutual situation that you and she are involved in. The co-worker can be an acquaintance, but not a good friend.

While at a party or get-together, approach an acquaintance of the opposite sex and compliment them on their behavior or appearance.

In a crowded restaurant, ask a stranger if you may sit at his table for lunch.

In an antique store, ask one of the patrons for their opinion on a particular item you are interested in and ask them to elaborate on their answer.

Offer assistance to someone who seems to need help, for example, if you notice a person standing on a corner looking at a map, go up and offer your help.

Go up to someone who is standing by themself during intermission at a play and start a conversation.

Initiate a conversation with the person sitting next to you at a lunch counter.

Start one brief (three minute) conversation the next time you are in the laundromat.

Initiate one conversation each day with a stranger and one with an acquaintance.

Initiate two conversations each day with strangers and two with acquaintances.

Keep track for three days of the opportunities you have to initiate a conversation with someone. Jot down each situation in a small notebook.

For each opportunity you have to initiate a conversation, give yourself no points if you say nothing, one point if you smile and make a brief statement such as "nice day" and two points if you make a longer statement which leads to a conversation.

The next time you are invited to a meeting or party, go up to two or three people standing together and enter the conversation.

Information to Evaluate Your Progress

Number of brief conversations (less than three minutes) initiated with strangers each week.

Number of conversations initiated with acquaintances each week which lasted at least 30 minutes.

Number of different ways you initiate conversations each week.

Number of conversations initiated at work each week.

Number of different people you initiate conversations with each week.

Percentage of times you initiate conversations when an opportunity arises.

Checklist

If you have difficulty initiating conversations with others:

- Perhaps you approach people before you have something specific in mind to say, and you hesitate, stammer, or otherwise feel embarrassed. It is helpful to think about what you are going to say before approaching someone, and you may even wish to covertly rehearse your response or to overtly practice it at home before trying it out. Prepare an initial comment in addition to a couple of related ones.

- Perhaps you approach people too abruptly, without any preliminary nonverbal contact, for instance, looking at or being next to them. Perhaps s(he) was startled, or perplexed.

- The way you delivered you opening remark may have detracted from your initiation, that is, maybe your voice was too loud or too soft, or your words were not clearly enunciated (Did the person say "uh?" or "what?" after your comment?); or you talked too fast or stuttered; or you fidgeted or glanced around furtively; or frowned and bit your lip. However, the warmth you transmit in spite of some of these behaviors (for example through smiles) may wipe away their possible negative effects.

- You may need more rehearsal before trying out new ways of initiating conversations. Rehearsal will help you identify problems in your delivery.

- You may use the same type of initiating remark in all situations. For instance, you may always ask others for advice or information as a way of starting a conversation. You will get bored using the same type of comment and this lack of enthusiasm might be perceived by others—and also one type of remark is not likely to be successful in all circumstances. To increase your impact in various situations, you could practice all eight ways of starting conversations.

- Perhaps you too quickly accept a minimal or less than enthusiastic reaction as a rejection and quickly terminate the interaction.

- Your appearance may not be appealing to those you would like to meet. If you were in situations where initiations from others were possible but no one came up to talk to you, perhaps you did not appear open to conversation. For instance, did you sit in a corner with your back or side to the center of activity, looking down at the floor, at the ceiling or in your drink? Did you look *at* people, did you smile? Or, did you scan the situation so quickly that direct eye contact with anyone was avoided? Did you look sullen and frown?

9

Maintaining Conversations

Learning new behaviors, such as initiating conversations with strangers and acquaintances, often requires more deliberate planning at first to insure success. It is a good idea to have several related comments (statements and questions) in mind that you can use after making an opening remark and to rehearse these before trying them out. You can elaborate upon your initial comment by using various combinations of the categories for initiating conversations described in the last chapter. By combining types of comments, you can construct a sequence of related remarks that can get a conversation off to a good start. Thus, what to say next is an extension of what you said first.

Examples of people who use one type of comment too frequently include the "flatterer" who is overly complimentary; the "interviewer" who asks questions of others without offering information in return; the "lecturer" who expounds on personal knowledge, opinions and feelings with little concern about listening to others; and the "complainer" who is full of bad things to say about the world.

A good rule to follow to insure a balance between talking and listening during conversations is to utilize both statements and questions. That is, after you elaborate on your own point of view (state what you think and offer some reasons why), ask about the other person's views, for example, "What do you think?" or "Have you found this to be the case?" Asking a question after you have expressed yourself is a direct invitation for others to speak. People enjoy conversations in which they are involved. In devising your own conversational sequences, keep in mind this "answer-elaborate-ask" rule or the "ask-listen-respond and elaborate-ask" rule.

Elaborating on Your Initial Remarks

- "Have you been waiting long too?" (Ask a question about a mutual activity)

    "Do you know when the doors open?" (Ask for information)

"I suppose waiting for something makes you appreciate it more."
(Humorous comment regarding a mutual activity)

"Do you think we have a chance of getting in?" (Ask for an opinion)

"Would you like to read this while you're waiting?" (Share something)

- "That was an excellent presentation." (Give a compliment)

  "You offered some new ways of looking at an old topic." (Elaborate on comment)

  "Have you given this presentation before?" (Ask for information)

  "Do you have any time now for a cup of coffee? I would enjoy discussing your talk." (Ask the other person to join you)

  "My head is buzzing with ideas and questions. For example . . ." (Share a personal feeling)

  "The entire audience was absorbed . . ." (Offer a compliment)

- "You look bored. Am I right?" (Make an observation)

  "Would you like some coffee?" (Offer something)

  "I saw you sitting here when I came in. Have you been here long?" (Make an observation about a person's behavior; ask for information)

  "Well frankly, so am I. Would you like to get some coffee?" (Share a feeling; ask the other to join you)

  "Have you heard this before?" (Ask for information)

- "Excuse me, what is that you're eating?" (Ask question about what the person is doing)

  "It looks really good. Last time I was here I had something similar." (Share a feeling and information)

  "I think I'll get one—may I join you?" (Ask to join the person)

  "It looks like a pastry my grandmother used to make." (Share an experience)

  "Where did you get it?" (Ask for information)

- "Would you like to sit here?" (Ask someone to join you)

  "Do you come here often?" (Ask for information)

  "It's really busy here today." (Comment on a mutual situation)

  "I'd really like the company." (Share a feeling)

  "Would you like to share a pot of tea? This tea is really good." (Offer something and share an opinion)

  "I noticed you when you came in. You seemed uncertain about staying." (Make an observation)

- "Excuse me. Could you help me with this?" (Ask for help)

  "I can't seem to manage both things at once." (Share a feeling)

  "I'm sure glad you came along. I was having quite a time." (Thank the other; offer a personal feeling)

"This job is driving me crazy." (Share a feeling)

"I appreciate your giving me a hand." (Thank the other)

- "Would you like a piece of gum?" (Offer something)

    "It's a new kind. I really like it." (Offer information; and an opinion)

    "Chewing is a great way to pass the time." (Offer a humorous opinion)

    "What type of gum do you like?" (Ask for information)

- "This discussion is really boring me." (Share an opinion)

    "Do you know how much longer it will last?" (Ask for information about a mutual situation)

    "He seems to talk in great generalities with no examples." (Offer an opinion)

    "I'm having a hard time concentrating on what he is saying." (Share a feeling)

    "Do you find his talk interesting so far?" (Ask for someone's opinion)

    (If yes) "What do you find interesting about it?" (Ask for an elaboration on an opinion)

- "Are you walking toward the university?" (Ask for information)

    "I'm going that way, too." (Share information)

    "It is really a pleasant walk." (Offer an opinion)

    "The sky is so beautiful today. It reminds me of a midwestern sky." (Share an opinion and information)

Once a conversation is initiated and a number of comments have been exchanged, you can do several things to encourage a longer and more interesting discussion. These behaviors can be divided into two broad categories: those that change the purpose, content or topic of conversation and those that create a more personal atmosphere.

Changing the Purpose of a Conversation

Changing the purpose, content, and specific topics can provide a refreshing lift to any conversation, even between old friends. The initial purpose of an exchange is often created by the situation in which the conversation was initiated. For example, your initial goal may be to discuss a problem related to work with a fellow employee. When discussion related to this has been completed, you may wish to shift the focus to a discussion of vacation plans. You could make a transitional statement and then introduce your new purpose. You might say, "Well, I think I'm clear about that now. By the way, where do you usually go for your vacation?"

Along with a change in purpose may come a change in the expectations of the participants in the conversation. The expectation that a conversation will be relatively casual may change if you attempt to alter the purpose to a more personal one. Perhaps the initial expectations of your exchange did not include the possibility of introducing more personal topics. A change in purpose may cause some initial uneasiness until the other person adjusts to the new emphasis. If you notice that someone continues to be uncomfortable, then you could redirect the conversation to its original goal. Several possible goals that a conversation might center on are listed below.

Pass the time until something else happens   You may talk with the person next to you in a theater line until the doors open and the performance starts. There are few expectations that the conversation is anything more than a prelude to a more central event.

Catch up on what has been happening   You might approach a neighbor after he has returned from vacation and ask him about his travels: "Well, hello, Carl, welcome back. How was your trip?"

A sexual prelude   You may engage in after-dinner conversation with a prospective sexual partner. You may say, "I'm feeling very happy right now. I really enjoy being with you."

Solicit help, assistance; ask a favor of someone   You might invite a co-worker to go out for coffee to ask her advice concerning a new idea you have related to your job. "Doris, I'd like your reactions to some ideas I have about improving the selection process. Do you have time to get some coffee and talk about it now?"

Find out how someone feels about you; solicit positive and negative feedback   You might ask an acquaintance out to lunch to discuss his impressions of your report at a meeting. "How about lunch today? I'd like to have some feedback from you about my report this morning?"

Have a good time; engage in "happy talk"   During the bus ride home after work, you might share a funny incident with the person next to you. "I know what you mean about fatigue. I was so tired today that I ate my lunch at 10:30 this morning just to keep myself awake. Then I fell asleep during my lunch break!"

Engage in a serious discussion about some issue   At a party, you might engage someone in a discussion concerning a current political issue. "What do you think about the new bill to offer medical insurance to everyone?"

Find out something about the person   Over coffee with someone, ask about her interests, goals, and so on. "It seems that you really enjoy your work. What kind of things do you like to do in your spare time?"

Share your experiences; engage in self-disclosure   In an art museum you might discuss your personal artistic views with someone you have just met. You should be somewhat cautious about discussing highly personal issues with strangers since this might be embarrassing to them. As a guideline, you may first want to think about how *you* would react if someone were to say the same thing to you.

Tell someone how you feel about him   You might phone an acquaintance to tell him how much you enjoyed his company and why, and express your interest in cultivating a relationship with him. "Hi Roger, I wanted to call and tell you how much I enjoyed being with you yesterday. I had a great time and I'd like to see you again soon. How about dinner at my place Thursday evening?" Or you may wish to express a negative reaction. Critical comments, especially with newly made acquaintances, need to be well thought out and carefully delivered.

Changing the Content of Conversations

You may not want to change the entire purpose of an interaction but only the content of conversation within the confines of the original goal. For example, if your objective is to seriously explore some area of interest, you may want to shift from a discussion of one issue to another rather than shift to "happy talk." Examples of several general conversational content areas are listed below.

Discussion of feelings, assumptions, or impressions of each other   This exchange can be employed when passing the time, seeking assistance, or learning more about someone. While having a conversation with the person next to you in a theater line, you might remark, "It sounds like you know a lot about classical music." Or, when seeking assistance from someone, you might comment, "I really appreciate your honesty about this, it makes it a lot easier for me."

Share personal thoughts and opinions about a subject   This content area can be used to catch up on what has been happening, engage in a serious discussion, and in self-disclosure. You might say, "I think your recent promotion has a lot to do with the added pressures you're now feeling."

Engage in a mutual exchange of facts; share objective information about a subject   This may be useful in passing the time or engaging in a serious discussion. For example, "To add to your point, I recently read that over 65 percent of those who start eventually drop out."

One person shares an area of expertise and the other listens and learns   This may be useful when the goal is to seek help, advice or assistance, engage in a serious discussion, or learn about someone. For example, "I'd like you to describe your experiences because I believe it will help me with my dilemma."

Share fantasies, dreams, images, goals or desires   This might facilitate a conversation if the purpose involves a sexual prelude, having a good time, or learning about someone. You might say, "I've always wanted to learn how to ski. I know I would enjoy the sensation of speeding down the slopes. How about you?"

Share recent activities   This area is useful if the conversational purpose involves having a good time, sharing personal information, or a sexual prelude. For example, "I had a very interesting experience this week. I was bicycling around the lake and literally ran into an old school friend of mine!"

Share past experiences   This can be employed when the goal of conversation is to seek advice or assistance from another, engage in a serious discussion, or share a part of your personal background with someone. You might say, "Your suggestion would have been appropriate about ten years ago when I was struggling with the problems of divorce and redirection."

Share humorous events, tell funny stories, laugh at yourself   This can be used to catch up on what has been happening and having a good time. You might say, "Since I saw you last, the funniest thing happened. Do you remember Bill from the office? Well, one day . . ."

Changing the Topic of Conversation

In addition to changing the purpose and content areas of a conversation to maintain an enjoyable exchange, you can also introduce new topics. You can change the topic of conversation without modifying the purpose or general content of an exchange. For example, if the overall purpose is to pass the time, and the general content involves sharing recent activities, specific topics could include what you did last weekend, the book you recently finished, and so on.

There are a variety of ways to introduce new topics. An ideal time to introduce a new topic is generally during a brief pause in the conversation which serves as a natural break between one topic and the next. You might say: "Yesterday I read in the paper that . . ."; "Have you heard about . . ."; "I've been wanting to tell you about . . ." Sometimes the relationship between several topics exists only because the mention of one happens to remind you of the other. You might say, "Speaking of . . . do you think . . ." or "That reminded me of the time when . . ." or "I know it doesn't seem related, but that reminded me of . . ."

Another way to change the topic of conversation is simply to say that you would like to discuss something else. If you become bored or irritated when talking about some topic, then you should change it. You could express your desire directly and perhaps give a reason. You might say:

> "Let's talk about something lighter for a while. What do you think will happen with the . . ." (This comment might also serve to change the *purpose* of the conversation from a serious discussion to "happy talk.")
>
> "I'm getting a little upset talking about this. I'd like to talk about something else."
>
> "I think we have exhausted that topic for a while. I wanted to ask you about . . ."

Preparation can increase your ability to introduce different topics of conversation. Determine several topics that you could introduce which interest you, and which you are either familiar with or would like to learn more about. Weekly news magazines and newspapers provide possible topics of conversation and you may find it valuable to read one of these on a regular basis. Topics could include: bicycling, shopping for a new car, opera, animal behavior, astrology, the presidential campaign, a particular TV program or film, horseracing, stock market trends and forecasts, bookbinding, recent bestsellers, endangered species, the fire in your neighbor's yard, and so on. It may be helpful to list each topic plus specific points under each on index cards for easy reference. If shopping for a new car is a topic of interest, you might list such points as: the models you like and why, repair records, safety features, gas mileage, and resale value. Two examples of itemized topics are provided below.

Topic: bicycle trip	**Topic: concert you attended**
You got lost	Where you sat
Length of trip	Interesting people you saw there
Unusual sights	Part of performance you liked best
Sunburn	Comparison with other concerts
Sore muscles	Bought a record of the concert

Once you have listed and itemized some topics that you can readily introduce, enjoy talking about, and can elaborate upon, you can use this list as a reminder before engaging in conversations. Remember to begin with relatively "safe" topics, those you feel comfortable discussing.

Examples of the relationship between specific topics and the content and purpose of a conversation:

Let's say the primary *purpose* of the conversation is to "pass the time." Various *content* areas might include discussing feelings and impressions about each other and sharing recent activities. Within the area of discussing feelings and impressions, *topics* might incude first impressions of each other, and your feelings and impressions about each other's work. These topics can be further refined into itemized points, as noted below.

Purpose: To pass the time
Content Area:　Discuss feelings, impressions about each other.
　　Topic:　Your first impressions of each other:
　　　　　　Positive impressions
　　　　　　Negative impressions, reservations
　　　　　　Your assumptions about their impressions of you
　　Topic:　Your feelings about each other's work:
　　　　　　It's importance in your lives
　　　　　　The amount of time required
　　　　　　The importance of recognition
Content Area:　Share recent activities.
　　Topic:　Your vacation:
　　　　　　Where you went
　　　　　　People you met
　　　　　　Pictures you took
　　Topic:　Antique show you went to:
　　　　　　Glassware
　　　　　　Brass beds
　　　　　　Oak tables

Purpose: Share your experiences with other person, engage in self-disclosure.
Content Area:　Share past experiences.
　　Topic:　How your family spent weekends:
　　　　　　Relatives
　　　　　　Camping
　　　　　　Sunday dinners at your house
　　Topic:　Your high school days:
　　　　　　Your friends
　　　　　　Beach parites
　　　　　　Clubs you belonged to
Content Area:　Share fantasies, dreams, desires.

Topic: Dream highlights:
   Flying
   Frightening episodes
   Seeing old friends in dreams
Topic: Your career fantasies:
   How you see the next ten years
   What you would like to accomplish
   Problems that might arise
   Exciting prospects to look forward to

Your comment may be answered with an unfriendly reply. Let's say you ask someone, "May I check out a reservation I have about you?" and s(he) says, "No, I really don't care what you think about me." You might say, "Well, that lets me know where you stand." There is no need to offer any excuses for asking your question; you do not have to defend yourself and should resist the efforts of others to force you into such a position. For example, the conversation above might continue:

Other: "What do you know about where I stand. People are always try-
        ing to figure out other people. They should let them alone."
You: "Perhaps this isn't a good time to continue talking. I think I'll get
        going."
Other: "That's another thing I don't like. Opening up a topic and then
        running off. Just like all the others."
You: "I can see that you're upset, but I still don't see any point in pursu-
        ing this discussion."

Sample Assignments

In a serious discussion following a lecture with someone you have just met, change the content from exchange of information about the presentation to sharing your childhood experiences with family camping.

During the next conversation you have with a new acquaintance, introduce two topics of conversation along with some specific points under each.

Let's say your interactions generally center around lighthearted joking and having a good time with an acquaintance at work. After you initiate a conversation during lunch, express your interest in finding out more about him, what his interests and ambitions are, and so on. Attempt to continue this conversation for at least one half-hour.

As you are passing the time with a stranger seated next to you before a concert begins, change your conversation from sharing your opinions on free concerts to your impressions about her.

After you have initiated and maintained a 15-minute conversation with a stranger, attempt to introduce a topic that is a little more difficult for you to discuss, for example, your political beliefs.

Initiate and maintain a five-minute conversation with an acquaintance or a stranger. (The exact duration should be just above what you now can do with ease.)

Go to the local bookstore and start two five-minute conversations.

Information to Evaluate Your Progress

- Number of conversations initiated which were at least 15 minutes long.
- Percentage of conversations in which you introduced at least one topic of conversation.
- Number of times you changed the purpose of a conversation with satisfactory results.
- Number of new topics you learned something about and introduced into your conversations each week.

Checklist

If you have trouble maintaining conversations:

- Was the new purpose of the conversation compatible with the situation?
- Did you attempt to change the purpose of the conversation too often?
- In changing the content area you may also have changed the purpose of the conversation when this was not desired by either you or the other person. If the purpose was to have a serious discussion, did you unwittingly change this objective by sharing a funny incident?
- Perhaps you ran out of topics to introduce. Did you enter the conversation prepared to discuss several different topics?
- Did you continue to discuss a topic despite negative reactions? Did someone seem nervous or hesitate to contribute?
- Perhaps you are not balancing talking with listening. Are you following the "answer-ask" rule? Are you balancing your own contributions with questions concerning the other person's point of view?
- The conversation may have become monotonous. Did you discuss a particular topic too long?
- You may wait too long to introduce a new topic in order to change a disagreeable or boring conversation. Your attempts to change the subject may be expressed with resentment and thus ignored or reacted to in a negative manner.

10

Ending Conversations and Arranging for Future Meetings

Increasing your social contacts also involves having to terminate conversations and arrange for future meetings more often. It is important for your conversational enjoyment to learn how to end conversations that you do not enjoy, prolong those which are pleasurable, be skillful in arranging for future meetings with people whom you would like to see again, and be firm in refusing requests for later meetings that you are not interested in.

The appropriate way to end a conversation is somewhat dependent upon whether you both remain in the same place, for example, during a party or intermission at a concert, or whether you can leave the situation, as in a conversation struck up on the street or in a store. In either case, you may see someone else whom you would like to talk to and say, "Excuse me, I see someone that I'd like to say hello to." If you can leave the situation, in addition to actually starting to move away, you could say "Excuse me. I have go now," or "Well, I think I'll continue my walk." It's a good idea to start your exit immediately. For instance, you could stand up, get your coat, and ease your way toward the exit. If you remain where you are and continue to talk, s(he) may not believe that you really want or need to leave. If you have invited people over to your home and feel that you would like to end the evening, perhaps because of tiredness or other commitments, you could offer a statement that implies your intent as well as indicates your enjoyment of the evening. You could say, for example, "I've really enjoyed this evening. I'd like to get together again soon."

Given that you do not wish to continue an exchange, you should remain politely firm. If the other person attempts to prolong an interaction by saying, "I'll walk with you," you might say, "No, I would prefer to walk by myself." There is no need to be harsh or rude in order to be firm. That is, one can be assertive without being aggressive. Don't allow yourself to be pressured into continuing an encounter when you do not wish to do so nor allow yourself to be "talked into" arranging a future meeting with someone when you would rather not.

Let's say you wish to terminate an exchange at a party as well as get something to drink. You could say "Excuse me, I think I'll get a drink." S(he) may offer to get this for you in which case you should acknowledge the offer but pursue your interests by saying, "No, I'd rather get it myself, but thanks for offering." If s(he) continues to follow you around even when you move away, more direct statements may be necessary to convince him/her that you are not "playing hard to get" and in fact want to be on your own. For example, you could say, "I'd really like to be on my own for a while; perhaps I'll see you later," or "I want to meet a lot of people this evening, so I'm going to move around and get acquainted. So long . . ." If further discouragement is necessary you might say, "Fred, I don't appreciate you following me around, I'd prefer to go my own way by myself." If s(he) persists, then you should turn away and start a conversation with someone else.

Learning to Say "No"

Saying "no" can be made easier in several ways. It is important to use the word "no" in refusal statements. Sometimes when people are not comfortable with being direct, they use many words and phrases in turning down a request without ever using the word "no." They may say, "Well, I just don't know . . ." or "I'm sorry, I don't think so . . ." Including the word "no" in your statement can be a signal that you have made up your mind and have no intention of changing it. When expressing refusal, look directly at the person, talk loud enough to be heard, and slow enough to be understood with a relative absence of stammers and hesitations. Your body should be oriented toward the person.

It is not necessary to offer a reason, although you may do so. It may be necessary to repeat yourself several times before the other person "gets the message." It's not necessary to come up with a new reason or statement each time you refuse; the original one is perfectly legitimate and may have more impact because of its repetition. Shorter refusal statements are often more powerful since they are direct and to the point. The more excuses you give, the more opportunities the other person has to persuade you by removing the reason for the excuse. If you say, "I have no phone," s(he) may reply, "Well, I'll just come over." The more reasons you give, the more difficult it will be for you to terminate the exchange. A reluctance to refuse unwanted requests may be related to a belief that you have to please everyone, that it is awful to hurt or disappoint people and that this should be avoided at all costs, that others have more of a right than you do to determine what you will do, and that saying "no" cannot be done in a nice way. Keep in mind that others have a perfect right to ask and you have a perfect right to refuse.

Avoid "getting rid of" someone by providing information about how s(he) can contact you, or by writing down telephone numbers or addresses when you have no intention of seeing someone again. Although giving such information may result in the other person leaving you alone at the time, you may have to deal with an unwanted interaction in the future. Also, it is a dishonest response. Often the best way to clarify and obtain what you want or don't want in relationships is to be honest and direct. This gives others a clear message of your feelings and intentions which can reduce discomfort due to uncertainty and ambiguity. Thus, when you wish to end a conversation and don't want to arrange for a future contact and say, "I must go," and someone asks for your phone number or a specific time to see you again, you might say, "No, I'd rather leave it open. I don't feel comfortable making future arrangements right now," or, "No, I don't usually give out my phone number, I'd rather leave it to chance."

People may attempt to influence you by trying to make you feel guilty by saying that you have hurt their feelings. Such attempts are really an infringement upon your rights and rather than making you feel guilty, a more appropriate reaction would be anger concerning their efforts to make you feel bad. For example, if you turn someone down for a request for a later meeting, they might say, "Gee, I really want to see you again. I feel bad that you won't see me." You might reply, "I can understand why you feel this way, but . . ." and then repeat your original statement.

A person may force you to escalate your reactions due to their refusal to accept your earlier attempts to express your preferences. The following illustrates an exchange that might occur when someone arrives at your home unannounced at a time when you would like to be by yourself.

Marsha:	"I was just going by and thought I would stop and visit."
Fred:	"Gee, I'm afraid you picked a bad time. I was looking forward to having this time to myself. Perhaps we can make it another time."
Marsha:	"The drive over was really hectic. Do you mind if I get a glass of water?"
Fred:	"Oh sure. Come into the kitchen."
Marsha:	(They return to the living room where she sits down.) "I'll just have to sit for a while."
Fred:	"Like I said. I was looking forward to having this time to myself. Perhaps we could arrange another time."
Marsha:	"How about taking a short break to talk to me."

Fred:	"No, I'd rather stick with my plans for the day. I really want to be by myself this afternoon."
Marsha:	"The hermit type, huh?"
Fred:	"Perhaps you could call it that. I'll have to ask you to leave now."
Marsha:	"Boy, you are really in a foul mood. Good-bye."
Fred:	"Good-bye."

Many people feel that it is impolite to maintain one's preferences in the face of repeated requests to alter them. On the contrary, exerting pressure upon someone is impolite. It is impolite to badger you and to be insensitive to your preferences.

Arranging for Future Contacts

Pleasurable interactions may be lost by neglecting to arrange for future contact. You may not know how to contact a person again. In other situations, someone may be in a given place at certain times, for instance, you both may have an evening class together. If this is not the case, then some minimal information must be exchanged. You could, for example, share how much you enjoyed the conversation, say that you would like to get together again, and offer your phone number and name, that is, write it down. You are then in a stronger position to request information, such as a name, phone number, and possibly an address. Some people are reluctant to give out their phone numbers but may be willing to accept yours. A variety of ways to obtain information are given below:

"Let's exchange phone numbers so we can contact each other."

"Let me write down my phone number and I'd like to have yours so we can reach other later."

"I have a place around the corner. Let me give you the address so you can stop by when you have time."

You may not wish to rely on the person to call you and so try to arrange another meeting. S(he) may feel more comfortable in seeing you again if the meeting place is on neutral ground, such as in front of a movie or a museum rather than coming to your house or going to his/her home.

If you want to set up a definite meeting, you might say:

"I have two tickets for _____ on Friday night. Would you like to join me?"

"I'm going hiking out to _____ this Saturday. Would you like to go with me?"

"How about coming over for lunch tomorrow?"

"I'm going to experiment with crepes this Thursday night. Would you like to join me?"

"I have to go now. I'd like to continue our conversation at another time. Can we meet here again tomorrow?"

You may initiate a conversation in a situation which is restrictive, uncomfortable or noisy, and want to continue it in a place more conducive to a pleasant exchange. Listed below are some examples of what you could say:

"Do you have time to continue talking over some coffee?"

"Let's go to a more comfortable spot."

"Why don't we walk down the street. It's noisy in here."

"My place is just around the corner. Would you like to come up and have some coffee?"

Your overture may be refused or met with a minimal or less than enthusiastic reaction. The person may make it clear that s(he) cannot continue the interaction at this time, but suggest that you exchange information so that you can contact each other later. If a reaction is noncommittal, that is, you can't determine whether someone is interested or not, you should pursue the matter by suggesting the exchange of information. You might say, "Well, I've enjoyed our brief conversation and would like to talk with you again. Would you have time for a cup of coffee around the same time tomorrow?" If the answer is still noncommittal, you could offer some information which enables the person to find you at a later time without putting him on the spot. You could say, for example, "Well, I have lunch at _____ just about every day. I hope I see you there when you have time." Potentially rich interactions may be lost if you hastily interpret noncommittal replies as rejection. They may not be and you should take the responsibility of checking them out. An example is presented below which illustrates what you might say when attempting to arrange for the continuation of a conversation. Several examples are included of how you could respond if the other person reacts to you in a less than enthusiastic way. For practice, you should think up your own examples. Let's say you have just met someone in a bookstore and after a short but enjoyable conversation you suggest continuing the exchange elsewhere by saying, "How about going down the street for a cup of coffee? I'm really enjoying our talk and would like to continue it in a more comfortable place." S(he) might say, "That's a good idea. Where do you want to go?" You might reply, "I was thinking of the coffeehouse on 15th Avenue. It's only a block up the street. How does that sound?"

S(he) might say, "I have to go now but I enjoyed our talk. Let me give you my phone number and let's get together again soon." You might respond, "That's a great idea! I'll give you mine too." S(he) might offer a minimal response such as, "No thanks, I have to go now." You might say, "I'm sorry to hear that, perhaps we can continue our discussion tomorrow. Will you be here around this time tomorrow?" Or, perhaps you might take more initiative by saying, "Well, maybe we can get together at a more convenient time. Here's my phone number. I'd enjoy hearing from you when you have more time." S(he) might respond in an obviously negative way, for instance, "No, I don't have any more time to just sit around and talk." You could reply, "I don't think having an enjoyable conversation is a waste of time, in fact, I feel my time has been well spent," or "Well, perhaps we can talk again when you *do* have more time. I'm in here quite often, perhaps we'll see each other again sometime."

If you would like to continue the conversation but notice that the other person appears distracted, in some situations you could offer them an opportunity to express their preferences by saying, for example, "I think I'll go over and get a drink. Would you like to go over with me?" This is more effective than assuming that s(he) is not interested.

Using the telephone   Telephone contacts are useful in terms of their being enjoyable in and of themselves and also as ways to arrange future meetings with others. These possibilities are related in that if you have an enjoyable phone conversation with a person, s(he) may be more interested in seeing you at a future time.

When you are telephoning a person you do not know well, you should give some thought as to what you will talk about before making the call. If you are calling to arrange a meeting, you should identify beforehand some interesting place to go or activity to engage in, such as a particular movie on Saturday night, or a bicycling trip on Sunday afternoon. In addition, have several dates and times in mind in case one is not possible for the other person. These should be suggested if the person tells you that s(he) cannot go at the time you first suggest. You could have in mind several movies at different times, or other activities for Sunday afternoon, such as going to a concert or taking a walk in the park.

If you are calling to arrange a future contact, it is not necessary to engage in lengthy preliminary conversation, although you could share some information about yourself. For example, if you spent the day gardening you might share this. Self-disclosure allows others to get acquainted with you as well as encourages them to share their activities with you, but make the purpose of your call clear at a fairly early point.

First, make sure that you are talking to the right person. Otherwise, you may make a number of statements to the wrong person and then feel embarrassed. When someone picks up the phone say, "Hello, is Richard there?" If he is not there, you can leave your name and phone number and ask that he call you, or you could leave a message that you called and find out when would be a likely time to reach him.

If you reach the person and you have just met briefly, it is important to identify yourself, perhaps by recalling where you met. Unless this is done, s(he) may not remember you. You might say, "Hi. This is Chris. We met at the art show the other night," and then pause to allow recognition of who you are. If you had exchanged last names, include this in your introduction and then introduce the purpose of your call. You might say: "There is a new art show that I have tickets for next Friday night and I thought you might enjoy going with me to see it. It is by . . ." Thus, you offer an activity in which you think s(he) will be interested, state what night it is happening, and describe it briefly. By having concrete suggestions in mind for things to do which may be fun, you increase the chances that your offer will be accepted, particularly if you speak enthusiastically about the event or activity. You yourself should be interested in it and convey this to the other person. If you present the idea in a low-key bored manner, the activity might not seem very appealing. It is important that you clearly state that you would like to go together. People sometimes make the mistake of not being clear about why they are calling. If you say, "There is an art show by _____ this Saturday night," s(he) might say, "Thanks for letting me know, maybe I'll see you there."

If your offer is accepted, clarify all important details of the future meeting, including when and where you will meet. You might say, "I'm really looking forward to seeing that movie with you Saturday night. How about if I pick you up at 7:00 p.m. at your place? That way, we can make the film in plenty of time," or if more neutral ground is desirable, "Why don't we meet in front of the museum at 2:00 p.m. this Sunday?" S(he) might say: "I'm sorry I can't. I have plans for that night, but it would be fun to get together." This is an open invitation for you to continue to make some plans.

Persisting in your request   If your first offer is not accepted, suggest an alternative, prefacing the statement with an indication that you would still like to get together and do something. For example, you might say:

> "Well, I thought it would be fun to get together and if you can't make the art show, how about going to the movies on Sunday night? There are some good shows around such as _____ which is playing at the _____. I've heard it's very good."

Thus, as mentioned earlier, do not take being turned down as a firm indication that someone is not interested in further contact with you. Other possible replies to your overture are illustrated below together with possible reactions.

S(he) may turn down your second suggestion as well. He might reply, "No, I have plans for that night too." You could say, "Well, it looks like you're really busy this weekend, would next weekend be better for you?" or "I'm still interested in seeing the show *and* seeing you again, how about a week night, say Tuesday evening?" If further invitations are declined or if you feel hesitant to pursue the matter in view of two refusals, you might repeat your interest in seeing her/him and say, "It seems you are pretty busy now. I'll give you a call in a week or so. I hope you'll have more time then."

It is difficult at times to determine whether or not someone is interested in you but is preoccupied or shy and so doesn't say much, or whether s(he) is disinterested. Such distinctions are easier to make if others share their feelings and intentions, for instance, they might say, "I'm sorry that I haven't been able to see much of you lately. I have been struggling with some problems. I'm still interested in our getting together," or, "I might as well be honest with you, I don't feel we have much in common."

Unfortunately, many people still feel uncomfortable with being honest and try to "get the message across" in indirect ways. However, despite the hesitation of others in being direct, you can take the initiative (it's up to you!) in determining the meaning behind minimal responses and being turned down. You might say, "Bruce, this is the third time that you have been unable to meet me for lunch. I'd like to know if you're really interested in seeing me again or whether I should stop calling, and I'd appreciate your being honest."

Someone may want to see you again, but not be interested in what you have offered as an activity or prefer to spend that time alone. S(he) might reply to your invitation by saying, "No, I'm really not interested in seeing the show," to which you could say, "Well, there are other things we could do. I'd enjoy visiting the new wilderness park just opened to the public recently. Perhaps we could go Sunday afternoon and take a picnic lunch. Does that appeal to you?" On the other hand, if s(he) said, "No, I'm really too busy right now to see anyone," you might say "I understand how a schedule can take over everything. Why not give me a call when you have some free time. I'd like to spend some of it with you." S(he) might let you know that s(he) is not interested in seeing you again by saying, "No, I really don't care to spend any time with you right now." You might reply, "I appreciate your directness, though I'm sorry you feel that way. Call me if you change your mind. Good-bye," or "Well, if you feel differently at a later time, give me a ring. But for now, I'll say good-bye . . ."

To reduce the possiblity of rejection, it's important that you try to arrange future contacts with people with whom you have had a pleasant interaction or who appear friendly. When you are developing social skills, it's especially important that you select people with whom an extended encounter is likely to be successful.

Responding to refusals   It is important that you learn to respond appropriately to being told "no." An appropriate reaction to being turned down includes a feeling of disappointment in addition to positive self-statements for trying to exert more influence over your social exchanges. You may say to yourself, "I'm sorry I won't be seeing him tonight, but at least I tried and it will be easier next time." You may also make a decision to try again at a later time. Any negative self-statements (self-criticism, putting yourself down, and overgeneralizing about yourself) should be re-evaluated (see Chapter 14). Development of positive self-instructions will help you cope with negative or harsh reactions from others as well as foster "gracious" reactions even to abrupt replies. For example, you may choose not to respond rather than lashing back at someone who turns you down in a harsh way. Either covert (in your imagination) or overt rehearsal of various replies to certain responses from others will help to prepare you for a variety of reactions. For example, you could record your own answers to each. Listening to your replies will offer you valuable feedback.

Sample Assignments

Try to practice each assignment below at least once. You may find that you can accomplish several during a one-week period, or you may space them out depending on your schedule, skill and comfort. Remember that practice is important in developing skill and comfort, and the more you practice, the more opportunities you have to observe what others do in social situations.

Arrange for a brief continuation of a meeting (fifteen minutes to one half-hour) with an acquaintance, for example, over coffee or a beer.

Same as above but with a stranger and, in addition, find out how you can contact them at a later time.

Arrange for a later meeting (at least one hour in length) with another person. Obtain his/her name and write down the details of your later meeting.

Arrange for an evening out with an acquaintance. Again, write down the details of your meeting. This meeting should be at least two hours in duration.

Telephone the person soon after your meeting (given that it went well) and arrange for another one.

Practice ending conversations with different types of departing statements using examples in the text as well as constructing you own.

Practice saying "no" in situations in which you do not wish to accept offers.

Information to Evaluate Your Progress

- Number of future meetings arranged and held each week.
- Percentage of times you turned down a request for a future meeting when you wanted to.
- Percentage of times you "tried again" to arrange a future contact after being turned down at first.

Checklist

If you have trouble ending conversations, arranging future contacts or avoiding unwanted meetings:

- You may not try to end conversations when you would like to. With very talkative people, remember that you may have to break into their conversation in order to excuse yourself.
- You may allow yourself to be trapped into extending conversations or arranging meetings because you do not maintain your preference when others persist.
- Perhaps you forget to obtain the information necessary to contact a person.
- You may not have interesting places in mind to suggest going to together, or not sound enthusiastic when talking about them.
- You may wait too long to try and arrange for a continuation of an exchange or to get needed information and therefore feel rushed and don't do as well.
- Perhaps you don't share something about yourself first. For example, tell the other person your name, offer your phone number, and tell her how much you enjoyed the conversation.
- You may give up too easily. That is, when first turned down, you may not ask again.
- You may ask for more of a commitment than someone is ready for. S(he) may turn down an offer to spend the day together but readily accept an offer to simply meet for coffee.

11

How to Change Your Participation in Conversations

You can learn to increase your participation in conversations by practicing elaborated opinion statements, breaking into an ongoing conversation, resisting interruption, and turning off talkative people.

Giving Elaborated Opinion Statements

An elaborated opinion statement begins with a personal pronoun such as "I," "me," or "my" and contains a compound sentence—several phrases connected by such words as "because," "and," "but," "therefore." An example is: "I think you're right because it's important to be very thorough in a case like this." This illustrates the basic type of statement you should concentrate on in this section—offering and elaborating upon your personal opinion.

There are several reasons why learning how to give such elaborated statements is important. People are more successful in increasing statements of opinion than other types of statements (such as asking questions or giving information). This makes sense when you think about it. There is a limit to the number of questions you can ask or facts you can offer before being considered an "interviewer" or a "lecturer." In contrast, opinion statements are often the "workhorse" of many discussions and you can increase their frequency without unpleasant consequences.

Also, opinion statements are easy to identify, which makes them easier to learn. They often begin with such phrases as: "I think that," "It seems to me that . . ." "In my opinion . . ." "I feel that . . ." and so on. Further, such statements provide a relatively safe way to contribute to a discussion. You don't have to have an irrefutable argument prepared and supported with lots of facts to express your ideas. And, it is not necessary to come up with an original thought or a perfectly phrased statement each time you want to say something. So, regardless of the topic, you can usually say something about it if you use opinion statements, even if it's only to comment, "I think your argument makes sense in light of my own experience." Elaborating on your opinions is important because very often people who don't take part much in conversations tend to make short statements. For example, they might agree by saying, "right," "uh-huh," or "I think you're right," instead of adding their own thoughts on the subject.

There are a variety of different types of statements you can give in a discussion:

"I think that's true and another example might be . . ." (Comment on what another person has *just* said)

"I thought what he said earlier was important because . . ." or, "I'd like to go back to your example about . . ." (Express an opinion on something said earlier)

"I agree because it seems to me that . . ." or, "I like your analysis because you seem to . . ." or, "I don't think that sounds like a good idea because . . ." or, "I disagree with part of your comment. I think that . . ." (Agree or disagree with what someone has said)

"Well, to answer your question, I think that . . ." or, "That's a good question. It seems to me that . . ." (Express your opinion in answer to someone's direct question)

"I think we should get back to the main point because . . ." or, "I believe we're off the track here, I see the main issue as . . ." (Change the whole direction or emphasis of the discussion)

Listed below are several examples of such statements. They are taken from a conversation concerning the problem of drug use in a neighborhood counseling center. Notice the use of the personal pronouns "I" and "me," and such words as "because," "and," and "since."

"I agree with you because I think that if the people who come to the center really need help, then they'll just have to follow the rules."

"I wish we could agree on whether we think the problem is serious or not, then we could proceed to decide what actions need to be taken to alleviate the problem."

"I was going to take the opposite position. That is, I think we should let the people who come to the center know exactly what the problem is."

You can obtain some practice in identifying elaborated opinion statements by circling the number of each comment in the following discussion that meets the criteria, i.e. those that *begin with a personal pronoun* and *contain a compound sentence.*

1. "I think we need to find out if there really is a drug problem so that we'll know what we're up against."

2. "Yeah, the problem is, how do we stop the use of drugs without alienating those who come to the center?"

3. "That's a good question."

4. "How do we find out how much drug use is going on, or is this part of the problem? How do we find out?"

5. "I think we should ask the people who use the center not to bring dope in because it will only cause problems."

6. "I was thinking that, too, but maybe they'll just laugh in our face."

7. "Why do you think they'll do that?"

8. "I just have a feeling that if we make a big production out of this, that we'll just make fools of ourselves, so maybe we should just keep quiet about it."

9. "If we keep quiet then we might get busted."

10. "What about posting a notice?"

11. "I don't think that would work because people don't pay attention to posted signs and notices."

12. "Well, I guess we'll just have to tell each person individually. For example, before we start to talk to each person about their problems, we could tell them not to smoke dope during the rap session."

There are six elaborated opinion statements in the discussion: 1, 5, 6, 8, 11, and 12. If you did not identify most of the statements correctly, review the previous section.

Practice   After you read each excerpt below, write down an elaborated statement in the space provided. Remember to begin with a personal pronoun. For example, you might say "I think," or "Well, it seems to me that." Your remark does not have to be an original idea. You can rephrase or summarize what another person has said, comment and then ask another question, or try to change the direction of the conversation.

1. "I think we need to find out if there really is a drug problem so that we'll know what we're up against."
Your response: _____
_____
_____

2. "What about posting a notice? But actually people don't pay attention to posted signs and notices."
Your response: _____
_____
_____

3. "Maybe we could also have people going up and down the hallway, looking into rooms periodically."
Your response: _____
_____
_____

In order to increase your participation in conversations, it is important to be able to talk for longer periods of time. Verbalize outloud your responses to each of the three written excerpts above and talk for increasingly longer durations. Time yourself starting with a 15 second interval on number 1. When you have fulfilled the time requirement, don't stop speaking abruptly, but complete your comment. Next try to talk for 30 seconds in response to excerpt number 2, and 45 seconds in response to number 3. It is quite normal for speakers to talk for durations of one minute in a real conversation. Having to speak for a specified amount of time may seem somewhat artificial at first, but such practice will help you to speak for longer periods of time in an actual conversation. Remember that valuable contributions to a discussion are often attempts to reformulate, refine, or summarize ideas already expressed.

Breaking into Ongoing Conversations

In addition to expressing more elaborated opinions for longer periods of time, it is also necessary to know how to get into an ongoing conversation so you can express yourself fully. To enter a fast-moving conversation, you may have to initiate your comments during a brief pause or hesitation. If you wait for a long pause, you may not be able to get a word in and the topic could change before you get a chance to share your ideas. This does not mean that you interrupt others while they are still talking, but rather, that you speak up quickly after they have finished their statement. Interrupting others indicates that you do not care about what they are saying and are only concerned with your own ideas. Therefore, instead of interrupting, it is important that you learn to identify when there is a *natural pause* in the conversation, when the person stops to breathe or collect his thoughts after a statement. Even a very talkative person must occasionally stop talking. Examples of taking advantage of natural pauses in a conversation and interrupting while the person is still talking are given below:

"And I think it would be tremendous if they could develop . . ."
    (interruption) "Yes, and I was thinking . . ."
". . . it before the year is out."
    (natural pause) "Yes, and I was thinking . . ."

It is also helpful to know how to enter the conversation when the opportunity does not present itself. You could raise your voice slightly. Even a slight increase functions as a signal to others that you want to speak. It is not necessary to yell or scream. The content of your speech, may also be helpful. Questions ("I don't understand what you mean by . . ."), opinions, and the use of the person's name are often good ways to enter a conversation. It is difficult for someone to continue talking nonstop if distracted by the use of his name, for example, "Ralph, I agree with what you're saying because . . ."

When attempting to break into conversation, what you do with your body can be just as important as what you say with words. Moving your body toward the other person, for example, sitting forward in your chair, or standing closer to the other person, may engage his attention. It is more likely that others will offer you an opportunity to talk if you sit in a visible location than if you sit crumpled in your chair fading into the shadows. Your hands can be used as expressive tools to distract and gain attention. Hand gestures can signal others that you wish to speak or a light touch on the arm or shoulder can communicate your readiness to speak.

The techniques for gaining entry into a conversation can be used when you want to enter a group of people who are talking, for example, at a party. First approach the group and position yourself as if you were a part of the group. Listen for a while so you know what is being discussed, and then gain the attention of the others by offering an opinion about what is being discussed or share an experience.

Resisting Interruption

In a lively discussion not only is it necessary to speak up quickly but it is also important to resist the attempts of others to interrupt you so that you can complete your comments. The more you talk, the more likely it is that others will attempt to cut into your conversation before you are done. One simple and effective way to resist interruption is to raise your voice slightly when someone attempts to break into your sentence. This signals the interruptor that you want to finish your comment before they speak. Raising your voice also helps you to maintain your train of thought during an interruption attempt. In fact, any technique that will keep you from getting flustered and forgetting what you were talking about will assist you when resisting interuption. Establishing very brief eye contact with the "interruptor" is also helpful because it lets the person know you are aware of their interest in contributing but that you intend to continue speaking.

Another technique that helps in resisting interruption is pausing very briefly and then repeating your opening phrase. Again, this is a signal that you have every intention of completing your statement, and it helps you to regain your composure and recall what you were going to say. Sometimes when you stop talking abruptly when someone interrupts you, they realize what they have done and apologize or at least keep quiet until you have finished your statement.

Another strategy for resisting interruption is to continue talking without hesitating or pausing when someone interrupts you. This may require a slight raise in voice volume as well as some "parallel" talking for a while until the person realizes that s(he) has interrupted and that you intend to finish your sentence. This technique can be difficult to use since many of us have been taught that it is "rude" to talk while someone else is talking. Yet, if you are the one who is being interrupted, you have a perfect "right" to complete your comment before giving up the floor.

Other techniques for handling interruption involve asking the person to wait or otherwise commenting on the interruption attempt itself. These may be more appropriate after other techniques have been tried. Various ways of phrasing such a request are illustrated below:

> "I can see what you . . . (Now, what about . . .) just a minute, I'd like to finish. I can see what you mean, but there's the problem of being too strict and uptight."

You could tell the person later that you have noticed that s(he) seems to interrupt you quite often and that this bothers you. Perhaps the person is not aware of his or her behavior or does not know what to do about it. If this is the case, you could suggest a cue or signal such as raising your hand slightly to alert him whenever he interrupts you. This feedback may help the person to change his behavior.

One way to discourage interruption attempts is to ignore them until you have completed your comment. If you are talking with several people, direct your comments toward the receptive ones and avoid eye contact with the interrupter. When you have finished, then you may wish to turn to the person and say, "(Name), did you have something you would like to say?" A hand signal indicating "stop" or "hold it" can be an effective adjunct to your verbal message of "please wait" or "just a minute." Or, a touch may bring attention to your attempts to resist interruption. For example, touching the person's hand or arm as you say, "(Name), I'd like to finish, please," can emphasize your desire to complete your statement while acknowledging the other person's interest in speaking.

You can also practice resisting interruptions by using a tape recorder as an interrupter. Record short segments of your own voice between recorded intervals of silence. You could record yourself saying, "Well, but I think . . ." and then pause 10 seconds and then say, "I see two other examples where . . ." and pause for seven seconds, and so on. Be sure to record variable periods of silence between interruption attempts so you won't know when to expect an interruption. Rewind the tape and play it as you express your opinions on some subject. You will be periodically interrupted by your own voice and thus have an opportunity to practice various techniques of resisting. Such rehearsal can be extremely helpful since you can try out different responses to see how they might work before you experiment with them in an actual conversation.

If you don't have access to a tape recorder, you could turn on a TV or radio at different intervals when talking out loud. This technique is not as effective as using the tape recorder because, you *know* when you are going to interrupt yourself and therefore you will be more prepared than if you were using the tape recorder. However, even this technique can provide some practice in experimenting with different strategies of resisting.

If you are able to get a friend to practice with, she can interrupt you at various times as you are talking aloud. You may want to instruct her to use short phrases at first such as "Well I . . ." "But what about . . ." so that you can experience success in resisting. As you become more skillful, ask her to make it more difficult by using longer phrases such as "Yes, but what about my idea for a new . . ." and interrupting many times during your comments.

You may find that even though you have attempted to break into a conversation and resist interruption several times, the other person still monopolizes the conversation. In that case, you can directly state your desire to speak by saying, "May I talk for a while?" or "(Name), I'd like to say something. I feel left out of the conversation," or "(Name), I would like to comment on your first point."

Another way to bring the person's attention to what he is doing is to stop looking at the speaker, stop smiling, stop nodding. This technique should be used sparingly because he may increase the amount of talk to regain your attention or he may get angry for being ignored. However, if used correctly, lack of attention can be a signal that he has lost your interest and should turn over the conversation to you or introduce another topic.

Decreasing Your Participation

You may feel that you talk too much when with others, or that you tend to monopolize discussions. Before trying to decrease your participation, be sure that you *do* talk more than your share. It may only seem to *you* that you talk too much, whereas others may not feel this way at all. To evaluate this, observe your next few conversations and try to determine if others have as much time to speak as you have. You may also wish to ask a trusted friend whether they think you tend to dominate conversations. If you discover that you *do* tend to monopolize, then some of the methods described below may help you to achieve a greater balance between talking and listening.

- Ask the other person for his opinion more frequently, being sure to wait for a response. For example, you might say, "What do you think about this issue?" (pause for an answer). Wait for the other person to finish speaking and for a brief pause before you speak to be sure you are not interrupting. Remind yourself that most people find it unpleasant to be interrupted and that your turn will come.

- Your problem may not be that you interrupt others while they are talking, but rather you may jump in *too* quickly after his speech stops, not allowing him to thoroughly finish what he wanted to say. You may mistakenly interpret a brief pause as an end to a person's speech when it may only be a transition from one sentence to the next. To prevent this, remind yourself to wait for a few seconds after his speech stops. You could delay your comments by covertly counting to three before starting to talk.

- To increase the other's participation, it is also important to provide positive feedback for their comments (see Chapter 13).

- Your comments may be too long and involved. If you find yourself telling long, elaborated stories, or citing twelve different examples to illustrate a point, or relating five years of your childhood experiences, this may leave others few choices except to listen or interrupt. If you notice that a person is quiet and looking around, this could be an indication that she is bored and that you are being long winded. If you find yourself being interrupted frequently, this may also mean that your comments are too long. To correct this, try to express yourself in shorter, simpler sentences and limit your examples, references and analogies. When you realize that you have been talking for a long time and that someone appears distracted or anxious to break into the conversation, you should stop talking and say, "Well, I guess you've heard enough from me on this issue. What do you think about it?"

- Another reason why others may not be as talkative as you would like is because you have been overly critical (see Chapter 13).

- When you are finished talking, look directly at the person. This can be a signal for her to begin talking. It is common for people to look around when they are talking, but it is important to bring your gaze back to the other person after you are finished speaking. If you look down at the floor or around the room after you have finished, s(he) may hesitate because s(he) did not get a signal to begin talking, perhaps thinking that you are not finished. You may mistakenly think that s(he) does not wish to speak and thus feel compelled to continue talking to fill up the silence.

Sample Assignments

Increasing Your Participation in Conversations

Count the number of elaborated opinion statements during a portion of your conversations over the next few days. If the rate is low, try to double this during the next week.

Try to express two elaborated opinions within one comment during each of your conversations. For example, "I think your idea is worthwhile because it takes many of the problems into account. However, I also think that my suggestion is worth considering because it reflects a different perspective."

Initiate a contact with an overly talkative person who usually monopolizes the conversation. Before the meeting, prepare a "script" of what you are going to say regarding his behavior, and express these comments during your exchange.

To practice breaking into an ongoing conversation, go up to a salesperson who is talking with another customer in a store, wait for a natural break in the conversation and then ask him a question.

Attempt to enter a small group discussion, for example, several co-workers having coffee together. Wait until you understand what they are talking about, and then attempt to join the conversation without interrupting anyone.

Arrange to practice resisting interruption with a friend.

Resist interruption in a conversation at least once by asking the person to please wait.

Resist attempts of a persistent interrupter by signaling with your hand that you would like her to stop cutting into your comments. Combine these gestures with a phrase such as, "Please wait."

Arrange to talk to a person who tends to monopolize conversations and practice the techniques discussed for turning off a talkative person. First, tell him that you would like to speak. If this does not work, try withdrawing your attention until he notices your inattention.

Decreasing Your Participation in Conversations

Ask the person for their opinions and ideas at least four times during your next two conversations.

In your conversations during the next three days, allow short periods of silence to occur before you begin to speak to make sure others have finished talking and have no more elaborations to make.

Information to Evaluate Your Progress

- Rate of your elaborated opinion statements during conversations five minutes or longer (rate per minute).

- Percentage of times you successfully resisted an interruption attempt.

- Rate with which you ask others for their opinion during conversations lasting five minutes or longer.

- Percentage of conversations in which you waited for a brief period after the other person finished speaking before you spoke.

Checklist

If you have trouble increasing your participation in conversations:

- Perhaps you hesitate too long to express your opinion, allowing the topic to change so that your comment is out of context. You may have to practice coming into conversations more quickly by expressing a short sentence at first just to get yourself into the conversation. For example, you might say, "Yes, I think that's true." The sooner you come in, the more likely you will be seen as a viable member of the discussion.

- Your voice volume and/or enunciation may be inadequate. Others may have difficulty hearing and understanding what you are saying, and therefore not react to your comments.

- Perhaps you hesitate to express your opinion because you do not see your ideas as unique. Keep in mind that being a worthwhile participant does not require you to come up with original ideas. You can be effective and influential by summarizing what others have said, offering additional examples for a point under discussion, and so on.

- You may communicate your desire to speak in overly subtle ways such as looking distracted or bored or sighing instead of directly expressing your interest in being more active in the discussion. Sometimes we expect others to "know" how we feel or what we want without taking the responsibility ourselves of making our desires known or acting directly to fulfill them.

- You may wait until you are angry to request your share of talk time. Express your desire before negative feelings build up.

- You may not directly confront an "interrupter" after more subtle approaches have failed.

If you have trouble decreasing your participation in conversations:

- Perhaps you do not attend carefully to others when they are talking (see Chapter 13).

- Perhaps you do not solicit the opinions of others.

- You may have to select some alternative behavior, such as counting to three to prevent you from jumping in too quickly before someone is finished speaking.

- Perhaps you are not sufficiently sensitive to the cues other people offer during discussions and so are unaware when you might be occupying more than your share of the discussion. Useful questions to ask yourself to heighten your sensitivity to someone's degree of interest include: Is she in a "listening posture"? Does she look interested? Do her comments encourage me to continue speaking?

12

How to Have More Enjoyable Conversations

Some people do not seem willing to go through the steps that are often required to get to know people who may possibly become close friends or lovers. Meeting new people, finding out how a variety of people live, and what they think may not seem enjoyable. You may only see them as a means to an end. If you do not have the skills to make these intermediate steps pleasurable, you are losing out on an important source of enjoyment in addition to reducing the possibility of forming meaningful relationships. Give yourself, and the other person, a chance. There are a number of ways to make such social contacts more fun.

Making Contacts Enjoyable

Be curious about people   The difference between the curiosity of children and that of adults about objects and people is striking at times. Children are full of questions while adults seldom ask questions about others. Try finding out, for example, what views people hold on certain issues, how they live, or what they do for recreation. There are a thousand dimensions of thought, feeling, and behavior that people may differ about, differences which might be of interest to you if you took the time to find out.

You might say, "Why should I bother?" Besides the fact that intermediate steps are often required in finding people who become important to us, there is an additional reason as well: you could learn something. Some people enjoy learning how things are done, or what experiences other people have had. Others enjoy talking about clothes, including finding out about materials and shops. Some people like to watch facial expressions and body movements. A number of ways to make contacts more enjoyable are discussed below.

Introduce topics that are of interest to you   You may blame a dull conversation on the other person when in fact you did not direct the discussion to something of interest to you. Perhaps you choose people who like to talk about things that don't interest you. Some degree of overlap in terms of topics you both enjoy talking about is necessary in order to have an enjoyable conversation. If you do not find a conversation interesting and try several times to change it but are unsuccessful, then you might consider ending it. There is no reason why you have to continue an unpleasant interaction.

Create a more personal atmosphere   Another way to maintain enjoyable conversations is to increase your "impact" by creating a more personal exchange. Ask a personal question or for a personal feeling; check out an assumption, impression, or observation you have made about someone; share a feeling you have about how someone affects you; reinforce others for specific behaviors that you like; state your impression of someone's reaction to you; express a reservation about someone, taking advantage of apparent differences and sharing your experiences. Some of these methods are illustrated below.

Check out an assumption about someone:

Ask for clarification before going further
"You seem to be well versed on this subject. Are you a writer?"
"You seem more relaxed now than when we first came in. Is that true?"
"You keep looking around and at your watch. Would you like to continue the discussion some other time?"

Express a reservation about someone
"You seem to view everything so negatively. Your pessimism is making me depressed."
"I wish you would express more enthusiasm about this."
"It bothers me when you say that."

Share your impression of how someone reacts to you
"It seems to me that you disagree with most of the opinions I offer."
"You seem to enjoy dancing."
"My sense of humor seems to confuse you at times."

Take advantage of apparent differences
"Your experience with . . . has been so different than mine, I'd like to hear more."
"Your opinion of . . . is the opposite of mine. Why do you think we differ so much?"

Share a personal feeling about how someone affects you
"Your comment really hurt my feelings."
"I feel very comfortable with you."
"I hesitate to share my feelings with you. I'm afraid you'll make fun of me."

Ask a personal question or for a personal feeling
"What is your personal feeling about this?"
"May I ask a personal question?" (Pause for a reply; if affirmative, then ask your question.)

Change negative thoughts to positive ones   Negative thoughts about yourself or others may interfere with the pleasure of your exchanges. For example, you may think, "This person is really boring," and make no attempt to change the direction of the conversation, or think, "I must sound stupid." You may hold irrational beliefs which interfere with your exchanges (see Chapter 14).

Express your opinions   You may not be as active as you could be in sharing with others what you think and why you believe certain things. If your conversations are imbalanced, with you always in a listening role, then you can increase your enjoyment by becoming more active. Be sure that you speak clearly and loudly enough so that people can easily hear you. Talking too softly or too quietly makes it hard for other people to follow what you say. If the strain is too great, they may give up listening and perhaps try to save the conversation by talking more and more themselves, or they may terminate the contact. If you talk too loudly, this may be embarrassing to others. The length of your comments should be adequate so that the conversation is stimulated. Too frequent, short, monosyllabic responses can turn a conversation into a question-answer format. To guard against this, elaborate when answering a question.

Be a good listener   Half-hearted listening in which you barely pay attention to what others say is not very interesting for anyone. If you frequently experience such a state, you can increase your enjoyment of conversations by giving the speaker more attention or changing the topic of conversation if it does not interest you. Active listening requires trying to understand what someone is saying as well as why s(he) is saying it in addition to thinking about the content in terms of your own beliefs. Active listening leads to questions which arise in your own mind about what is being said which form the basis of questions or comments when you next speak.

> Ask *questions* about or *paraphrase* what the other person has been talking about. These responses demonstrate your attentiveness and stimulate others to elaborate on their comments. You might say, "Do you mean you had to wait all that time?" or "It sounds awful!" Being a good listener makes it easier to increase your participation in conversations as your comments will be relevant to what 's being said. Also, ask the other person for his/her opinions. This encou ges him to share his views. Your request for his opinions demonstrates your interest in what he has to say, as well as making it easier for others to introduce their ideas. You might say, "What did you do then?" or "Why do you think that?" Poor listeners rarely ask questions of others, and really don't care about the answers to questions they do pose. Interrupting, of course, should be avoided. If you notice that someone has become overly quiet, you may have interrupted too often and thus discouraged him from talking.

Active listening also requires a posture of listening in which you face the person, look at him/her and offer encouraging smiles and head nods. We are not encouraging you to constantly smile or constantly look at others, but to offer this kind of feedback frequently enough to indicate that you are listening. If you smile too much, you may dilute the value of this behavior so that it will not mean much to others. Or, someone could think your smile is quite unrelated to whatever s(he) is saying. Also, too much eye contact may make both of you feel uncomfortable. Facial expressions are extremely important in conveying reactions. In fact, it has been reported that your attitude about someone is communicated 55 percent by facial expressions, 38 percent by vocal cues, and 7 percent by the verbal message. Your body position also reflects your reactions. It is probably more reinforcing to the other person if you face him/her and even lean your body forward a little than it would be if you sat or stood facing away or leaned back so far as to create a conversational distance between you. Slumping, sitting or standing far away, drumming your fingers impatiently on a table, or leaning back with your arms folded in a manner that communicates defiance or defensiveness will not encourage others to continue speaking. A message of "warmth" is often conveyed by combining direct eye contact, a smile, and a shift of posture toward the other person. However, we encourage you to keep an appropriate distance from the speaker. What is appropriate seems to vary from culture to culture. In America, a distance of one and a half to two feet when talking to an acquaintance or stranger is typical.

Being a good listener also includes providing verbal *indications of attentiveness* in the form of single words or short phrases while you are listening such as, "Uh-huh," "I agree," "Yes," "I see," "Right," "Good," "Wonderful," "That's great," "That's imaginative," and so on. It's certainly not necessary that you express such comments at the end of every sentence offered by the other person; this might become too repetitive, tiresome, and distracting to both of you. An occasional "Right" or "uh-huh" is appropriate.

Offering positive feedback   Your reactions to other people's comments may either encourage or discourage further sharing on their part. In addition to the encouraging behaviors mentioned above, such as asking others for their opinion, it is also important that you *express* your agreement with what others say if you feel it. Mutual agreement on opinions can provide one form of positive feedback to others. Don't allow your agreement to remain implicit. You could say, "Yes, I was thinking the same thing," or "I agree with what you just said." And, if the person *does* something that you like, express your reactions. You might say, "I love it when you laugh" or "I'm so glad you were here to help me with this." Making your positive reactions explicit in relation to what others do can enhance your exchanges.

Compliments may concern physical attributes such as telling a person who has lost weight how good he looks. Touching can be another expression of positive reactions. You could, for example, lightly touch the shoulder, arm, or hand of the person when accentuating a point or giving approval. If you enjoyed the conversation, tell the person before the exchange terminates. You could say, "I really enjoyed talking with you," or "I've had a good time with you this afternoon." Be sure your nonverbal behavior matches your verbal messages. For instance, if you tell someone how much you have enjoyed the conversation but look down at the floor without even a hint of a smile, it is unlikely that s(he) will believe you.

Negative reactions to be avoided include frowns, eye squinting, tightly pressed lips, looking away or around the room, or shaking your head in disapproval. Often, these gestures are unintended, that is, you may not be aware that you are engaging in them. Heightening your awareness of your nonverbal reactions will help you to eliminate those that impede an enjoyable exchange.

Sarcasm and name-calling should also be avoided. Unless you know the person fairly well and can predict his reactions, it might be well to avoid such remarks as, "A three-year-old could have done better than that." Like sarcasm, name-calling may have humorous intent, but its interpretation as "humorous" may not be shared by the person involved. It is wise to forego the use of such words as "dummy," "fatty," "tightwad," and so on. Words and phrases that can have a negative effect include: "You're so indecisive." Notice that many of these comments are accusatory. Also, they are dogmatic, as if you "know it all."

Accepting positive feedback   Learn to accept positive feedback others offer to you. If someone says to you, "I like the way you said that," simply thank him. Avoid comments which deny the basis for the compliment such as, "It was nothing."

Make use of your sense of humor   Most people enjoy laughing and many people obtain satisfaction from making others laugh. If you spot an opportunity to interject some humor, do so, given that the humor is not at someone else's expense.

Be an upper, not a downer   Another way to view conversations is in terms of the frequency of negative and positive statements made by each participant. Some people engage mainly in positive statements, that is, they talk about things they like as well as why they may like them. In contrast, others tell you how much they dislike certain people, policies, and so forth. These individuals are very skilled in negative opinions. How we talk about ourselves, or other people or events, affects our mood as well as other people's. Pick out the positive aspects of what is being said and talk about these. Avoid complaints. This does not mean that you should totally avoid discussing negative things, only that you give a preponderance of positive comments.

After your interactions with others, ask yourself whether you offered an enjoyable experience to the other person. This is not to make you feel self-conscious about the impression you made or did not make, but purely to assess whether you have given an enjoyable experience to another person. Ask yourself if *you* enjoyed the conversation. If so, it may be helpful to try to identify some of the specific reasons why you enjoyed the exchange so you can attempt to duplicate your behavior. If you did not enjoy the discussion, try to identify why this was so and pinpoint things you could have done differently. You can then try to alter your behavior in accord with this information during future conversations.

Avoid topics that make you uncomfortable   The topic of conversation may make you uncomfortable. You may mistakenly introduce such a topic or, more often, the other person will bring it up. Rather than allowing yourself to become increasingly uncomfortable, take the initiative and change the subject (see page 77). Of course, you may wish to gradually include topics that make you somewhat uncomfortable so you can become more relaxed when discussing such subjects. Start with ones that make you just a little anxious.

If someone is persistent in wishing to discuss a topic after you have indicated an interest in changing it, be sure to hold to your refusal. You may simply repeat your original request to change the topic. There is no need to offer excuses. Perhaps the person will even become accusatory by saying, "Gee, you're really uptight." In reply you might repeat part of your original statement, such as, "Right now I don't feel like talking about that."

Don't be afraid to admit that you don't know something   Sometimes other people assume that we know more than we do. Let us say that you are a gardener and are talking with someone you have just met who asks you about some flowers that grow in a different part of the country, about which you know nothing. Rather than trying to make something up or feeling that you have to supply some information no matter how minimal, you could simply say, "I've never heard of those flowers. There are so many varieties that it is hard to be familiar with them all." It is possible that an accusatory reply might ensue, such as, "I thought you were a gardener." You could say "Yes I am, but I'm just not aware of the ones you mentioned. I'd enjoy learning about them. What are they like?" In this response you ask the person for information while at the same time responding nondefensively. Important points to bear in mind when confronted by accusations, labels and other impolite comments, is to remain firm. Do not allow others to manipulate you into doing something that you don't want to do—whether it's talking about a certain topic for five minutes or spending hours with someone, and do not allow the comments to upset you or make you defensive, although with some people, whatever you say at a certain point may be interpreted as a defensive comment.

Handling silences   The first thing to keep in mind about silences is that they do not necessarily indicate that the conversation is dull and disinteresting. They often offer a refreshing pause in the conversation and there is no need to rush to fill the void in conversation. A silence offers a perfect opportunity to introduce another topic of conversation.

Dealing with criticism   You may initiate a conversation with someone who is very critical of you or your opinions and may address this directly. Avoid reactions which are hostile, defensive, which hedge or counterattack. You may admit the possiblity that the criticism may have some foundation even though you think it's unfair by saying, "That may be true, but . . ." and then clarifying your opinion if this has been the cause of the critical remark. Or it may be most appropriate to strongly reject the criticism.

Dealing with questions you do not wish to answer   Just as you have a perfect right to ask questions that are appropriate, you have a right to refuse to answer questions. Here, too, there is no need to offer excuses, and if the person is persistent, you have simply to say, "I don't want to discuss your question any further." People may assume that because they have shared certain information with you that you must do likewise. You are not obligated to reciprocate. If asked, "Well I've told you all about my problems. Now tell me about yours," you could say, "I'll tell you about a problem that came up at work today." This is a more competent response than saying, "I don't know you well enough to talk about my problems."

Dealing with anger   Inappropriate anger as well as inappropriate anxiety can dampen enjoyment during encounters. Thus if you find that you become angry when someone disagrees with you or when you are turned down after asking someone to meet you later, you should learn to change this reaction. An angry reaction in such situations is often based on a double standard of what is allowable. You may feel that you have a right to express opinions and ask other people for later meetings, but not offer them reciprocal rights to express their opinions and say "No" to you. So the first step you can take to alter your reactions is to question the reason for your anger.

The second step is to learn how to handle such situations differently. You can use positive self-instructions to change your reaction such as "There is no reason I should be angry now," "Just take it easy," "Getting angry won't help anything." As with anxiety, it is important to view anger as a *series of stages* rather than an all-or-nothing reaction over which you have no control. You may prepare for a provoking event by figuring out what you'll do and say in advance, or you may deal with your anger during the situation itself, and offer yourself positive self-statements afterwards. For example, when you successfully control your anger you could say, "That wasn't so bad, I really felt better not being angry." We are not saying that you should never feel angry and at times express this, but if you get angry often, perhaps you should take a look at the basis for your anger.

Dealing with a reply which appears dishonest   Let's say you think someone you are talking to is quite distracted and say, "You seem to be distracted. Would you like to talk about something else?" and the other person says, "Oh no, not at all. I was really enjoying our conversation." This statement may be contradicted by his behavior. You could at this point make a statement about your feelings such as, "(Name), I still feel that something else is on your mind," or you could change the subject. It usually does little good to pursue an honest answer with someone who is not willing to talk about their behavior. If you do pursue it, a gentle nudge will be more effective than an aggressive attempt which may make the other person defensive.

Finding out that someone is unavailable for certain types of relationships   What if you are interested in establishing contact with a woman with whom you might develop a relationship and during your first conversation you find out that she is romantically involved. You might say, "I didn't know. My loss, his gain." There is no need to apologize. A positive reaction entails being pleasant about the circumstances. And you shouldn't rush off or abandon the person abruptly.

Calls for reassurance   At times people make a bid for reassurance, for example by saying, "Sometimes I feel uncomfortable in social situations. Do you ever feel that way?" Simply replying, "Sometimes," is not very supportive. A more reassuring answer might be: "Sometimes, but I enjoy talking with you." Or perhaps someone says, "I think I talk too much." Rather than throwing it back at the person by saying, "Why do you say that?" you could offer reassurance by saying, "I sometimes do too, but I'm interested in what you're saying."

Learning to Calculate Possible Risks and Pleasures

Taking risks such as initiating a conversation with a stranger or offering your opinion will make your social contacts more enjoyable and lively. The risks you take should be in accord with how difficult various behaviors are for you in terms of their possible consequences, starting with ones where possible costs are small. One thing to learn is to risk the displeasure of others. If you are constantly worried about your "image" you will not be able to have very pleasurable interactions. One exercise to help you assume more risks is to carry out "mini cost-benefit analyses" in which you size up the possible benefits and costs of performing a behavior against those entailed in not performing it.

Let's say you are thinking about starting a conversation with a stranger sitting next to you on the bus. Possible benefits from trying to initiate a conversation might be meeting someone new, practicing your skills for initiating conversations, and having an enjoyable conversation. A possible cost might be receiving a negative reply. If you did not try, the possible benefits would be lost. People often overestimate the risks involved and underestimate the losses involved from a failure to act.

The suggestions mentioned above involve you in taking a *more active role* in conversations. If you ask yourself what you found of value in the conversations you had during the day and how much you enjoyed these, and the answer is not too encouraging, reflect back upon *your own* behavior in terms of what could be changed to increase your enjoyment.

Listed below are examples of positive verbal and nonverbal responses that you can practice and use in your interactions with others. Also listed are words and expressions that may have negative effects on others. Examine your own behaivor to identify ways in which you could be more positive in your exchanges with others.

Positive Reactions: Behaviors to Increase

Verbal Behaviors

Express words and phrases which indicate attentiveness, such as, "Yes," "I see," and so forth.

Express your agreement when you feel it.

Tell others when you like something they do.

Ask others for their opinions.

Ask questions about and paraphrase what others share with you.

Express your enjoyment of the conversation when you feel it.

Speak loudly enough. Make sure people can hear you easily.

Try to speak expressively rather than in a flat manner.

Try to speak fluently, that is, without a lot of hesitations.

Nonverbal Behaviors

  Smiles.

  Eye contact.

  Nods.

  Postural orientation toward others.

Negative Reactions: Behaviors to Decrease

Verbal Behaviors

  Strong criticism or disapproval.

  Sarcasm.

  Negative name-caling.

  Interrupting.

  Repetitive "filler" words such as, "You know."

Nonverbal Behaviors

  Frowning.

  Shaking head movements indicating disagreement.

  Looking away from the other person.

  A postural orientation away from others.

Sample Assignments

  Ask one appropriate personal question in each conversation you have over the next week.

  Introduce two topics of conversation that interest you during the interchanges you have during the next two days.

  Make the other person laugh at least once during the next five exchanges you have.

  Compliment someone at least once during the exchanges you have over the next week.

  Find out why a person believes a certain thing. Remember, the reasons why people believe what they do is often more interesting than what they believe.

  Include three positive comments and not more than one negative comment on what you are talking about during your conversations.

  The next time some topic bores or distresses you, change it to a more interesting one.

  Practice two different ways to admit your ignorance and then solicit information in some area that you're familiar with during your next five exchanges.

Check on your understanding of what another person is saying by paraphrasing what s(he) said at least three times during your conversations.

Increase the number of times you smile during your interactions.

Increase your eye contact with others when talking or listening to them.

If you make dogmatic statements, it may help if you record the number of such statements you make each day and then replace them with statements that begin, "I believe that . . ." "It seems to me that . . ." rather than "I know that . . ." or "It's a fact that . . ."

Decrease critical comments you make about what others say.

Share an interesting experience you had recently during each of your exchanges.

Decrease the number of times you please people at your own expense (when you really don't want to).

Take care not to interrupt others.

Information to Evaluate Your Progress

- Percentage of your exchanges where you made the other person laugh.
- Percentage of times you found yourself really interested in what another person was saying.
- Rate of compliments you offer others.

Checklist

If you are not having enjoyable conversations:

- Perhaps you expect your conversations to be enjoyable without any effort on your part.
- Perhaps you do not listen to what others say.
- Perhaps you engage in too much negative talk.
- You may not "personalize" the content enough. Perhaps you have shown no interest in someone by reinforcing her for specific things that she does that you like and asking appropriate personal questions. Or perhaps you do not share enough information about yourself.
- You may allow yourself to be manipulated into talking about things you don't want to discuss or become defensive. You may need to practice saying "no" and responding nondefensively to accusatory remarks.

- You may have irrational beliefs which interfere with your enjoyment of social exchanges and should re-evaluate these.

- Are you interested in offering the other person an enjoyable experience as well as yourself?

- You may be going overboard with a behavior, that is, smiling too frequently or looking so long that others become uncomfortable.

- You may not have increased the frequency of a positive behavior enough. Instead of not smiling at all during your exchanges, you may have increased to once every thirty minutes. Try to be more generous.

- Perhaps you increased your positive behaviors but forgot to decrease negative ones. Perhaps you are now smiling as you frown so that the latter dilutes the effect of your smiles.

Disagreeing with Others and Expressing Negative Feelings

You may find that you have difficulty expressing an opinion that differs from that of others, or, that when you *do* express a different opinion, it leads to an argument. You can learn to express differences of opinion in ways which are less likely to result in negative reactions. Disagreement can be buffered if delivered in a mild manner and if it acknowledges the other person's point of view.

Appropriate Disagreement

An appropriate or *assertive* disagreement involves expression of your own opinion or feelings on a particular subject without criticizing or negating the other person's point of view and, if possible, with recognition of areas of agreement and mutual concern. The use of elaborated opinion statements can make this easier such as, "That's an interesting point, however I disagree because . . ." Elaboration is important because it helps others to understand your perspective more fully and increases the likelihood that your opinion will be given adequate consideration. Disagreements that do not include elaborations may appear unduly abrupt.

Elaborated opinion statements are likely to be more acceptable than declarative or dogmatic statements such as, "This happens to be the way it is" or "Well, the *facts* show that . . ." which may be considered "aggressive" responses. Aggressive comments involve putting others down, criticizing them, embarrassing them, engaging in name-calling, and so on. Such comments may gain your objectives but they do so at the expense of others and usually involve a high "price" such as counter aggression from others.

Some Examples of Assertive Disagreement

Several examples of how you can phrase disagreements in an assertive manner are presented below. Notice that the comments often involve acknowledgment of the other person's position in addition to the expression of your own point of view. Notice too, that some of the examples attempt to point out areas of similarity or points of agreement in addition to bringing up differences. This helps to prevent others from becoming defensive and reacting negatively.

> "I think we both agree that the issue is important but I still think that . . ."
>
> "I wonder if another reason might be that . . ."
>
> "I disagree, (Name). I don't believe that plan would be workable because . . ."
>
> "You might consider this point . . ."
>
> "That's an interesting point of view, but have you ever thought about it this way . . ."
>
> "I feel differently. My experiences haven't shown that to be the case. For example . . ."
>
> "It sounds like we both agree that such a program would be beneficial, but we seem to differ in how to develop it. I think that . . ."

It is best to wait until someone is finished expressing his point of view before you disagree with it, unless you feel that you are not being given your share of talk time. If possible, however, wait for a natural break in the conversation. If you interrupt someone to express your difference of opinion, it is likely that they will react in a negative way to the interruption itself which may preclude any thoughtful consideration of your ideas.

Inappropriate Disagreement

It's inappropriate to attack another person by name-calling or to act as though his/her opinion is worthless. Avoid such statements as these:

> "You just don't know what you're talking about, you're ignorant of the facts . . ."
>
> "That's really a stupid idea. You have no idea of the consequences of your proposition . . ."

In contrast to assertive and aggressive responses, a "nonassertive" reaction to a difference of opinion would involve not saying anything at all—that is, keeping quiet about apparent differences, giving in to the other person's point of view, or offering indirect resistance. Examples include: "Well, I don't know . . ."; "Do you really think so?"; or "Uhm" when you mean, "I don't agree."

Handling Anger

It is important to share your differences as they arise rather than waiting until you become angry. Not only does anger impede the delivery of your disagreement, but it also stimulates others to become defensive and increases the likelihood of an argument. To avoid a build-up of anger, it is important to identify the initial signs of irritation that can accompany disagreement. These may include a slight increase in bodily tension or the occurrence of negative thoughts about someone. Perhaps your nonverbal behavior communicates anger or annoyance as you express an otherwise gentle verbal message. Did you raise your voice noticeably? Did you tense your body, frown, or put your hands on your hips? Try to be aware of what your body and facial expressions are communicating when you disagree. If you notice incongruities, practice delivering your disagreements in a milder manner. For example, try speaking in a quieter, slower voice; or assume a relaxed position.

An argument may ensue in spite of your attempts to express disagreements in a timely and assertive manner. If a particular topic or subject area becomes emotionally laden and compromise appears impossible, and the discussion seems to be accelerating into an argument, then you have a right to express these observations and to suggest that you move on to another topic. You might say:

> "_____, it really sounds like we've reached an impasse here. We both seem to have very strong feelings about this issue. I'd like to table this discussion for now and talk about something else, OK?"

> "This discussion seems to be edging on an argument, and I don't want our conversation to end on a negative note. Let's change the subject. (Pause) I was wondering about an earlier comment you made . . ."

Avoid persistent attempts to persuade or change the other person's point of view. Unrelenting disagreement with the goal of changing another's mind can become very unpleasant. It is a good idea not to run a discussion of differences "into the ground," but rather to acknowledge a standstill and go on to other topics unless you wish to end the conversation.

If your point of view changes after a discussion of differences, share this with the person. Expressing a change of opinion can be very positive to others and can enhance their impression of you as a flexible, thoughtful person. It can also prompt others to feel equally free to share more of their thoughts with you. You might say:

> "Talking with you has helped me to clarify some issues. I find that I'm beginning to question my original idea about . . .'

"Your argument is a good one and I find myself rethinking some of my initial ideas . . ."

Occasional disagreement can heighten the enjoyment of an exchange if you can disagree in a polite manner. You have as much right as others to express your views.

When someone listens to your disagreement or makes attempts to understand your point of view, support him for this. If you would like people to be tolerant and open-minded, then it's important that you pay attention to and comment on their efforts. You might say: "_____, I'm really glad you heard me out on this issue," or "It's refreshing to talk to someone who is open-minded and willing to consider other perspectives."

Expressing Negative Thoughts and Feelings

The most positive way to alter an offending behavior is to support a positive alternative. For example, if you dislike someone dropping over unannounced, when s(he) does call before coming over you could tell her how appreciative you are that she called first. Or if someone tends to interrupt you, you could tell them how good it felt to complete your thoughts before s(he) started to speak. Most people (if not all) would rather be praised for something positive they do than criticized for something you do not like. However, at times these positive attempts may fail or you may be faced with behavior you consider so negative that you feel it appropriate to point it out directly. You may, for example, ask someone who persistently interrupts you not to do so. You may want to tell someone that their persistent disagreeing, belittling remarks or criticism is unpleasant and irritating. If you try to ignore your discontent, hoping it will go away or that the other person will "take the hint" and change, you probably will become angry or hopeless about the situation improving, and reduce contact with them. We often make the mistake of assuming that others know when they bother us. Fortunately, or unfortunately, few of us can accurately "read" the minds of others. When more positive efforts have failed, expressing negative thoughts and feelings honestly and directly without putting others down in the process is important in establishing and maintaining relationships.

Choose the right time   There are a variety of things you can say and do that are *assertive* rather than aggressive or submissive expressions of negative feelings. If you are bringing up an issue that took place at an earlier time or in another situation, you may want to arrange a time to discuss it. You may not have expressed a concern at the time because of a lack of privacy or time. You might say, "I'd like to discuss something that's been bothering me. Do you have time now?" or "I'd like to talk about what happened last Tuesday. How about having lunch with me today?" Try not to surprise the person with your feedback when they may not be prepared or willing to hear you out. Thus, the *timing* of your comments can be crucial to the outcome of your attempts. The other person should have the opportunity to say, "I'm really not up to talking about it right now" or "Sure, I'm glad you brought the issue up." Avoid criticizing someone in front of others. If there is sufficient privacy and time to share your feedback, then it is usually a good idea to express your dissatisfactions as they arise rather than allowing them to build up.

Share responsibility   Focus upon the specific positive alternative that you would like when sharing your thoughts and feelings. This way you share responsibility for improving the situation. The other person is not left alone to struggle with trying to identify what to do differently. For example, rather than saying, "You're really thoughtless," meaning you do not introduce me to your friends, you should say, "I would like you to introduce me to your friends when we meet. When you don't I feel hurt." This informs the person what you would like him to do differently, and you take responsibility for your own feelings, and do not blame him for "making" you react in certain ways. Using vague statements that reflect blame are more likely to result in defensiveness and counter-blame than statements that express a *personal* dissatisfaction, which identify specific desired changes. It is important to use personal pronouns ("I," "me," "my") when expressing your dissatisfactions rather than the accusatory "you," which connotes blame. It would be better to say, "It bothers *me* when you say . . ." instead of, "You always say that I'm so and so . . ." or "*I* feel uncomfortable when you do such and such" instead of, "*You* make me so uptight when you . . ."

You may feel only a sense of irritation or disappointment and find it difficult to come up with specific examples. However, it is important to give enough thought to your dissatisfaction so that you identify what you would like to see more or less of, and to plan how to express your desires in a positive way. You may find it helpful to prepare a "script" of what you will say. Avoid name-calling, derogatory comments, and other "loaded" words. Such statements as, "You're so inconsiderate, cold, crazy, intolerable, paranoid, uptight, unfair," and so on, will interfere with a reasonable discussion of grievances and stimulate countercharges and putdowns.

Be serious   Give negative feedback in a serious and thoughtful manner. Try not to giggle, smile or laugh when rehearsing your response or when expressing your comments in actual exchanges. You could practice expressing them outloud, perhaps in front of a miror, and notice your nonverbal behavior. Do you smile and wring your hands? Rehearse your response until you feel comfortable with it and display appropriate gestures. If you smile and shift your position a lot, you broadcast your uneasiness and nervousness and appear unsure of yourself and others may think you are joking and not take you seriously. There is no need to apologize when giving negative feedback. Keep in mind that you have a right to express your feelings as long as it is not at the expense of others. If your feedback is well thought-out and skillfully expressed, there is no need to say you are sorry.

Practice beforehand   You could tape-record your statements and listen to them. You could even prepare for different reactions including hostile ones by recording these and rehearsing a reply. If the expression of your feeling is followed by a hostile or defensive reaction do not become defensive or back down. You may repeat your statement in the face of such a reply, or elaborate on your comment. Let us go back to the example mentioned before where you say, "I'd appreciate your calling me at least 30 minutes before coming over." A reply might be: "That takes all the sponaneity out of things. I wish you wouldn't be so rigid." You might reply, "I'm sorry you feel that way, but I would like that much notice before you come over. I might be involved in some work and not want any visitors."

Share your discomfort   When giving negative feedback, it is acceptable and, in many situations, helpful to share your own feelings of discomfort. Saying, "This is difficult for me, but I do want to talk to you about it," may put someone more at ease knowing that you are honestly struggling with being direct. It also shows your own fallibility and humanness. Self-disclosure is important in communicating that you are vulnerable too and do not see yourself in a "one-up" position. It is important to reassure the person that you still like them and want to maintain your relationship (if this is the case). For example, you might say, "Well, I'm glad I talked about it. I feel better. And I think our communication will be better in the future. I really appreciate your openness and flexibility." You could also point out (if it is true) how good it is that the two of you can discuss the differences you may have.

Our focus upon identifying positive alternatives and upon expressing desired changes in a positive manner should make it clear that expressing many criticisms of another person should be avoided!

Sample Assignments

Call up a friend or acquaintance and, during the conversation, disagree once on some subject that is not particularly critical or threatening.

Over the next week, recognize the other person's position before you offer your own views and be sure to say why you disagree.

During the next week, write down dogmatic or rude disagreement statements of others so you will become more sensitive to such comments.

During the next week, note when you felt like expressing a disagreement but did not and use these situations to practice what you could have said.

After initiating a conversation with an acquaintance, disagree once on a topic such as inflation, U.S. involvement in foreign disputes, government-supported child care facilities, or some other controversial subject.

Express your negative feelings when someone does something which you find annoying in a way which indicates that it is you who is bothered.

Practice responding in different ways to someone's negative reaction to something you say. You could, for example, offer a supportive comment such as, "I'm sorry you're upset."

Information to Evaluate Your Progress

Total the percentage of times you disagreed when you felt like it.

Percentage of times you expressed your negative feelings in a positive way (without blame and emphasizing a behavior to be increased).

Checklist

If you have trouble disagreeing:

- Perhaps you do not recognize the other person's position or elaborate upon your difference of opinion. You may simply say, "I don't agree" or "That's interesting, but I still don't accept your argument."
- You may wait too long to express your disagreement and thus react with anger and frustration.
- You may interrupt others in order to express your difference of opinion. Try to wait a few seconds after the person finishes his comment before you offer your point of view.
- Perhaps you do not show the other person that you appreciate her attentive listening to your views.

If you have difficulty giving negative feedback:

- You may laugh or giggle and the person may not take you seriously.
- You may not have taken the time to identify specific alternative behaviors that would improve the situation.
- You may phrase your statements in a blaming way rather than indicating that it is *you* who is disturbed.

- Perhaps you back down when the other person challenges you rather than remaining firm.

- Perhaps you depend too much on nonverbal "cues" such as coughing or sighing to indicate your dissatisfaction and wait for someone to ask you, "what's wrong?" Remember, it's up to you to take the initiative and to express what is bothering you.

- Perhaps you choose inappropriate times and places to discuss issues of concern.

- Remember that positives in an interaction should outweigh negatives. If you are finding fault with another person, perhaps you are being overly critical.

- You may accumulate small annoyances until they build into an arsenal of anger that may overwhelm someone. Share your reactions one at a time, as they come up.

14

Decreasing Troublesome Thoughts: The Use of Positive Self-Instructions

Negative self-statements such as, "I'm not very interesting," or visual images which depict unpleasant outcomes may interfere with effective and enjoyable exchanges. Having such thoughts or images when anticipating a social exchange may even result in your avoiding an exchange. A preoccupation with negative thoughts about yourself reduces your chances of making any interesting contribution to the conversation. You may not only discourage future contacts, but you may encourage further negative self-statements such as, "He really didn't like me," or, "I really *am* a boring person."

Negative self-statements and images can generate anxiety which further decreases your effectiveness and enjoyment of conversations. What we say to ourselves affects how we feel. The relationship between discomfort in social situations and negative self-statements is highlighted by a study showing that men who are anxious in social situations underestimate their ability to perform well and usually overestimate the negative results of their performance compared to men who are at ease in social situations. Men who are anxious making social contacts usually recall more negative self-evaluations which affects their present social behavior. This tendency is strengthened by their infrequent attempts at self-reinforcement.

Those who date less frequently have more negative and fewer positive self-statements than people who date regularly, but they do not differ from the latter group in knowledge of appropriate behaviors. Becoming aware of negative self-statements and learning to generate positive self-statements was found just as effective as coaching and rehearsal in increasing dating skills. These findings point to the importance of positive self-statements in relation to effective social skills and the need to assess one's internal dialogue in social situations. If you have a high frequency of negative thoughts, you should attempt to replace these with positive self-instructions.

Identifying Negative Thoughts

The first step is to identify the negative self-statements you make. Let's say that you are thinking about going over to a person and starting a conversation. Your sequence of thoughts may be as follows: "I would really like to meet him. I haven't seen him here before. But what would I say? I would probably stammer and stutter and make a fool of myself. He might think I'm a pushy woman." Even if you have initiated a conversation and have made a good impression, you may say afterwards, "See, I never should have done that. It was just a waste of time." You may not be aware that you are being negative or speculating upon dire outcomes. You may simply experience the discomfort such thoughts induce. This discomfort can make you aware of what you say to yourself on such occasions. Negative self-statements may concern your physical appearance ("I bet I look awful today"), your performance when with others ("I bet I am boring him"), or your perception of what others think of you ("I bet she thinks I'm really dumb"). It is helpful to keep a log for a few days in which you note when you experience anxiety in social situations as well as the related thoughts and images that occur at such times. This will also help you to identify the range of situations in which these negative thoughts occur. Perhaps these only occur when you get turned down, or think about getting turned down, or when you disagree with someone. Perhaps you have a habit of worrying that you will faint or spill your drink all over you.

Learning to Cope with Negative Thoughts

Each procedure described below teaches you an active coping skill which offers you more control over your thoughts and consequently over your discomfort level. You can learn positive self-instructions in stressful situations and are encouraged to view negative thoughts and discomfort as occasions to employ coping skills rather than, as in the past, to convince yourself of your helplessness and the unpleasantness of your anxiety. What previously functioned as a cue for discomfort and further negative self-statements is used for the opposite aims—to increase positive self-instructions and comfort. It is important that you learn to view anxiety as a series of stages rather than as an all or nothing reaction over which you have no control.

Meichenbaum* has offered the following examples of positive self-statements that may be helpful in anticipation of, during, and following encounters. (The word "stressor" means either a situation or person who may induce anxiety.)

Preparing for a stressor
>What is it you have to do?
>You can develop a plan to deal with it.
>Just think about what you can do about it. That's better than getting anxious.
>No negative self-statements: just think rationally.
>Don't worry; worry won't help anything.
>Maybe what you think is anxiety is eagerness to confront the stressor.

Confronting and handling a stressor
>Just "psych" yourself up—you can meet this challenge.
>You can convince yourself to do it. You can reason your fear away.
>One step at a time; you can handle the situation.
>Don't think about fear; just think about what you have to do. Stay relevant.
>This tenseness can be an ally; a cue to cope.
>Relax; you're in control. Take a slow deep breath.
>Ah, good.

Coping with the feeling of being overwhelmed
>When fear comes, just pause.
>Keep the focus on the present; what is it you have to do?
>Label your fear from 0 to 10 and watch it change.
>You should expect your fear to rise.
>Don't try to eliminate fear totally; just keep it manageable.

Reinforcing self-statements
>It worked; you did it.
>It wasn't as bad as you expected.
>You made more out of your fear than it was worth.
>Your damn ideas—that's the problem. When you control them, you control your fear.
>It's getting better each time you use the procedures.
>You can be pleased with the progress you're making.
>You did it!

Notice that there is a variety of positive self-instructions. Some refocus you on the task at hand and some focus you on relaxing. Others entail relabeling a situation (for example, maybe what you think is anxiety, is eagerness); seeking information, anticipatory problem solving, rehearsal; altering attributions (for example, rather than being mad at someone for upsetting you, realizing that *you* have allowed them to upset you).

Re-evaluation of Negative Thoughts

Ellis* has long advocated examining the basis for negative self-statements and points to their role in generating anxiety and interfering with enjoyment; that it is not events themselves which generate anxiety, but the thought we have about them. Some of your statements may reflect irrational beliefs. The thoughts "I don't think she likes me," may stem from your belief that "Everyone *must* like me." Clearly this is not a reasonable premise, as it is almost impossible that any person will be liked by everyone. A variety of such thoughts that he has identified are listed below.

> The idea that it is a dire necessity for an adult human being to be loved or approved by virtually every significant other person in his community.
>
> The idea that one should be thoroughly competent, adequate, and achieving in all possible respects, if one is to consider oneself worthwhile; that you should never make a mistake.
>
> The idea that certain people are bad, wicked, or villainous and that they should be severely blamed and punished for their villainy.
>
> The idea that it is awful and catastrophic when things are not the way one would very much like them to be.
>
> The idea that human unhappiness is externally caused and that people have little or no ability to control their sorrows and disturbances.
>
> The idea that if something is or may be dangerous or fearsome, one should be terribly concerned about it and should keep dwelling on the possibility of its occurring.
>
> The idea that it is easier to avoid than to face certain life difficulties and self-responsibilities.
>
> The idea that one should be dependent on others and needs someone stronger than oneself on whom to rely.
>
> The idea that one should become quite upset over other people's problems and disturbances.

Lazarus and Fay* have identified other irrational beliefs which may hinder enjoyable social contacts, including the belief that the less you disclose about yourself the better; that you should feel guilty if you act upon your preferences and others become upset; that you should not take risks; that you can draw general conclusions about others from individual statements or actions on their part; that your own peculiar thoughts are to be taken seriously. If you believe that you should disclose as little about yourself as possible, then you will withhold your feelings, experiences and opinions from others and they will not get to know you nor will you have the satisfaction of sharing yourself with others. You may fear that others will not like you if you disclose information about yourself. This in turn may be related to the belief that you must be liked by everyone.

The belief that you must be right will distract you from discussions and probably cause you to impose your opinions upon others. You may be drawn into extending interactions with others because of the guilt you feel about saying "no." Or you may believe that it is best not to take risks, and so you lose out on many opportunities. Drawing hasty general conclusions about others will close you off to finding out more about them because you have already categorized them. You may mistakenly believe that the "wierd" thoughts you have (such as what if my eyes cross when he is looking at me) are to be taken seriously rather than simply saying to yourself "that's a silly thought" and refocusing on your conversation.

When analyzing your negative thoughts be sure to carefully define each important term in your statement. If you say to yourself, "I'm really a failure" define what you mean by failure and why you are one. Defining your words will help you determine how you could prove or disprove your statement, and point the way toward changing your attitude. Statements may reflect a hasty judgment with no basis in reality. If someone you are talking to is very quiet and you say, "I guess s(he) thinks I'm dull," you might be misjudging her reaction. Ask yourself, "What is the basis for this statement?" S(he) could be quiet due to some reason unrelated to you, such as not feeling well, or being preoccupied with some other matter. Questioning yourself will help you determine the correctness of your observation. Even if you can muster up reasons to support your statement, there is a further question you should ask which is, "So what?" What dire events will befall you if you are boring someone? Perhaps the worst thing that could happen would be that he calls you "stupid" and slams the door in your face as he walks out. At least you're still in one piece and you're rid of someone who is rude.

These two criteria (the rationality of the statement, and the implications if the statement were true) are helpful to consider when trying to identify negative self-statements. For example, if you say to yourself "I must look awful today," the irrational aspect of this thought may rest on the assumption that "I must look good every day or people won't like me." You could challenge the implications of looking awful by saying to yourself, "If I don't look as good as possible, so what? I still have something to offer, and people with genuine interest in what I have to say won't be affected by superficialities." Examples of positive counterparts to negative self-statements are offered below:

Negative Self-Statement	*Examples of Positive Counterparts*
• "I bet I am really boring him."	• I think I've been saying some interesting things," or "You can't please everyone."
• "I must look awful today."	• "I look OK today." "I still have something to offer."
• "Oh dear, that was a stupid thing to say."	• "Everyone says things that aren't too well thought out at times."

- "I don't think she likes me."
- "I think she does like me." Or, "I know I am a likeable person."

In re-evaluating your negative thoughts, the following steps should be helpful:

1. Identify the anxiety you feel when in an exchange.
2. Specify and examine what you are saying to yourself that may be related to your discomfort, and realize the self-destructive role of negative self-statements. This step includes the examination of the rationality of these thoughts. Have you made hasty negative judgments? Do you have irrational expectations such as, "I want this person to really fall for me immediately." Try to become aware of the exact nature of any realistic statements you make and carefully re-evaluate them using the criteria described above.
3. Substitute positive self-instructions and say them to yourself.
4. Note any resulting decrease in anxiety. This will highlight the relationship between discomfort and negative thoughts.
5. Re-involve yourself in the conversation. This last step is important. If you don't redirect your attention to the conversation at hand, you will probably continue to think about your feelings. Interesting and enjoyable conversations are those which involve your total attention.

Rehearse this method before trying it out in actual situations. First identify some social situations in which you feel discomfort and have negative thoughts. Write each one down on an index card, noting the situation and what you say to yourself. Start with situations which create small amounts of discomfort and work up to those which induce more. You could use the subjective anxiety scale developed by Wolpe, to rank each item in terms of how much discomfort it produces. This ranges from 0 (very calm) to 100 (very anxious). For example, you may feel somewhat anxious when initiating a conversation and give this a rating of 15 units, but feel greater discomfort when trying to arrange a future meeting and give this a rating of 50.

During rehearsal, close your eyes and try to imagine yourself in the situation and reconstruct the things you say to yourself as clearly as possible. Then, still imagining yourself in the situation, re-evaluate these statements. Continue this re-evaluation, including the presentation of more reasonable thoughts until your discomfort decreases. After successfully reducing anxiety and replacing negative self-statements with positive self-instructions in this way, you can then progress to a more difficult situation and rehearse this. You may have to practice any one scene a numer of times before you can easily reduce your discomfort. An example of what someone might say when practicing is given below. The situation illustrates a man feeling discomfort when telling a woman that he would like to see her again.

Negative statement

"If I tell her that, she will think I am overeager, hard-up, and then I will really mess up my chances. Also, if she doesn't tell me that she would like to see me, then I'll feel awful since this means she doesn't want to see me again, ever."

Re-evaluation

Telling her that I would like to see her again is not such a big deal. It might please her very much and also I am honestly expressing my feelings. If she does not reciprocate by saying she'd like to see me, that doesn't necessarily mean she never wants to see me again, at least I have stated my feelings, and I should reinforce myself for trying. If I don't try, I might miss a really enjoyable experience.

Re-evaluation of your thoughts during conversations may be initially distracting. This effect will dissipate as you become more skilled in this procedure. However, until that time you may wish to use one of the methods described below during exchanges.

Use of Positive Self-Instructions Without Re-evaluation

This procedure involves identification of a negative self-statement or anxiety and using this as a cue for positive self-instructions which refocus your attention upon the exchange: what is being discussed, what the other person is saying or doing, how s(he) looks. For example, you might wonder what she does for fun, or what she thinks about a given topic. If you use this procedure and find no change in your discomfort or frequency of negative statements then you should combine this with re-evaluation of such statements.

Rehearse this procedure before you use it during exchanges. You should close your eyes and clearly imagine the situation, including what is said, what you think and feel, as well as your positive self-instructions.

A self-instructional method developed by Wolpe* involves saying the word "stop" to yourself as soon as a negative thought chain begins. Rehearsal can provide experience. Imagine situations in which negative thoughts arise. First say "stop" out loud, and then, after succeeding in stopping such thoughts in this manner, practice saying "stop" just to yourself. After you "stop" your negative thoughts, be sure to redirect your attention to the task at hand through positive self-instructions.

You may have negative images in social situations rather than negative thoughts. You may imagine spilling your drink all over yourself and people snickering around you; or going up to a small group of people who are talking together and imagine them looking at you scornfully. Noting what is going through your mind when you feel uncomfortable in social situations will help you identify whether you have negative thoughts, negative images or both. The procedures described above can be employed to learn how to substitute positive images for negative ones. A negative image can serve as a cue for positive images. For example, if you are thinking of starting a conversation with someone and you get an image of them ignoring you, this negative image should be a cue to instruct yourself to imagine a positive image, such as walking over to a person who greets you in a friendly way and saying hello. It is important to stop negative thoughts or images as soon as they occur and to do so consistently. The more you practice stopping these and replacing them with positive self-instructions, the more influence you will acquire over negative thoughts and images.

As you become more adept in influencing your behavior through positive self-instructions, you should experience less uncertainty and more enjoyment with others, and become a more interesting and enjoyable person to talk to.

Troublesome Thoughts About Others

The above discussion focused upon self-statements concerned with doubting yourself, feeling self-conscious, and paying too much attention to what other people think about you. Negative thoughts about *others* may also interfere with your enjoyment of conversations. Such thoughts include making swift derogatory judgments about others or blaming them for dull and disturbing conversations. You may feel uneasy, irritated, or bored and you can use these feelings as a cue to examine your thoughts.

Such thoughts not only interfere with attention to what others say and do, they also prevent you from improving the exchange. If you blame the other person, you may not try to alter the situation. Some examples of negative thoughts about others are given below together with possible counterparts.

Interfering Thought
- "This person doesn't know what he is talking about; he's an idiot."

- "This conversation is a bore. In fact most conversations bore me; they're not worth the effort."

Positive Counterpart
- "Maybe I can learn something if I listen. I wonder where he got such an idea; what makes him believe this?"

- "Having an enjoyable conversation is the responsibility of both parties; which means *me too*. If the encounter is boring I should change it."

You can use the procedures described earlier to decrease negative thoughts about others. For example, saying to yourself, "I wonder where she got that dumb idea," or, "This conversation is boring," can cue you to think, "I should do something about it." You can ask her why she holds a certain opinion, perhaps telling her of your disagreement; or introduce a topic that interests you in an attempt to change a boring conversation.

Sample Assignments

For one week keep a log of social situations in which you feel anxious, including what you say or imagine to yourself at these times. Such a log should include the date, the situation (who was involved, what you wanted to do, what you did), negative thoughts and images and any positive self-instructions you used.

Practice re-evaluating negative self-statements for 15 minutes each day.

Keep track of the number of positive self-statements you make during the first 15 minutes of each conversation during the next three days.

Re-evaluate negative thoughts you have during your conversations over the next week.

Use thought-stopping when you have negative thoughts or images in social situations during the next week; be sure to refocus your attention upon the conversation.

Keep track of the percentage of conversations you have each day in which you are able to decrease discomfort and negative thoughts or images by offering positive self-instructions.

See how many times you "catch yourself" having fun during a conversation rather than worrying about your image.

Some helpful assignments have been suggested by Lazarus and Fay:*

Keep track of how often you *allow* other people to upset you.

Each time you have a thought which strikes you as weird, such as "What if I start screaming?" practice saying to yourself, "It's only a thought," and refocus your attention upon the discussion you are having.

Keep track of how often you put yourself down as a person instead of criticizing one particular behavior. For example, rather than saying "I can never do anything right," you say, "I did not do that particular thing right."

Keep track of how often you falsely attribute your own feelings to external events rather than realizing that it is how *you* choose to respond to these that affects your feelings.

Make note of every time you negatively label your behavior and try to decrease this.

Sample Assignments for Decreasing Negative Thoughts About Others

For three days keep track of the percentage of conversations in which you have negative thoughts about others.

Practice developing positive counterparts to negative thoughts about others during your conversations over the next three days.

Select two positive things you like about each person you talk to during your next five exchanges and write them down afterwards.

Keep track of the percentage of conversations where you took steps to make the discussion more interesting, for example, by changing the topic.

An assignment suggested by Lazarus and Fay is:

Keep track of how often you put someone else down as a person rather than commenting on the specific source of your displeasure; You would say "I did not like the way he said that"; rather than "He is stupid."

Information to Evaluate Progress

Percentage of times you caught yourself having positive thoughts while talking to others.

Percentage of times you were able to eliminate negative thoughts and offer positive self-statements.

Average number of positive attributes you noted in others during your conversations.

Number of times you allowed someone to upset you.

Rate of positive thoughts about yourself.

Checklist

If you have trouble decreasing negative thoughts:

- Perhaps you cannot identify when you are anxious. You may not be aware of increases in anxiety that can be used to identify related negative thoughts or images. You may have to learn to become more aware of physical signs of anxiety (see Chapter 15).

- You may not have taken the time to identify the exact nature of the negative thoughts you have when you experience anxiety in social situations. This may make it difficult to select effective positive self-instructions.

- Perhaps you have not thoroughly examined the sources of irrationality of your judgments. You may have to ask yourself the following questions more often: "So what if _____ is the case? What is the worst thing that could happen?"

- Perhaps you have not identified believable positive self-statements. It is not necessary or even desirable to create fantastic statements about yourself in order to counteract negative thoughts. For instance, if you say to yourself, "I must be a boring person," it might be more believable to say, "I am an interesting person when I talk about my hobbies," rather than "I am a fantastic conversationalist on all topics."

- You may need to practice more before trying out the procedure in real life.

- You may find it distracting to re-evaluate your thoughts during encounters and should use another method when in social situations until you gain more skill in "re-evaluating" negative thoughts "on the spot."

- Perhaps you are having trouble narrowing down the negative thoughts because you have so many. You could select two which you find particularly troublesome and focus upon these. As you achieve skill in coping with these, select two others.

- You may not employ the procedure frequently enough. You may have to arrange a cue to remind yourself to counter negative thoughts.

- Perhaps you steadfastly hold some beliefs which are impossible to fulfill such as, "Everyone must like me."

- You may forget to refocus upon the discussion you are having.

- Perhaps you have not identified the situations in which you experience discomfort and have negative thoughts. This will make realistic practice difficult because the situations remain vague. The more realistic the practice periods, the more carry-over there should be to actual situations.

- You may be unable to identify your negative thoughts. They may be so automatic that you are not even aware of them. Keeping a careful log will help. Asking yourself the quesiton, "What am I thinking right now?" or "What am I saying to myself?" when you are feeling anxious or unhappy will make identification of negative thoughts and images easier.

- Perhaps you fail to select positive self-instructions which encourage you to be responsible for attempting change such as, "I'm getting bored with this topic. I'd better introduce another one."

*see Bibliography and References

15

Feeling More Relaxed with Others

There are many reasons why you may feel uncomfortable when meeting people. If you experience anxiety even though you have effective social skills, know when to perform them, and can cope effectively with negative thoughts, then you may benefit from learning one of the procedures described in this chapter. They are designed to reduce *physical tension*. These methods, however, will not be effective in removing anxiety associated with a lack of effective skills.

They will provide you with coping skills in social situations. After you learn *how* to relax, saying the word "relax" will have more influence over your tension level. You can use these methods to give more power to positive self-instructions such as "stay calm." They will also increase your ability to identify the early stages of anxiety so you can use your coping skills at this point rather than waiting until anxiety reaches a high level.

Progressive Relaxation

Progressive relaxation training enables you to become aware of muscle tension, and teaches you how to decrease this tension. Muscle tension is focused upon because many people who experience anxiety have increased muscle tension.

The general practice is to tense and then release major muscle groups while paying close attention to the differences between tension and relaxation. Initial practice sessions may require about forty-five minutes, but as you acquire skill you will be able to attain a state of relaxation much more rapidly, say in one minute. You can then start relaxing from whatever point of tension that already exists. It is helpful to use a word such as "relax" when you change from a tensed to a relaxed state so that this word will later serve as a cue to relax.

The same procedure is followed for each muscle group. You first tense a group and hold the tension for about five seconds while noting the changes in sensation that take place. Then you immediately release the tension upon saying a cue word such as "relax."

Be sure to attend to changes in sensation, noting the difference between tension and relaxation of the muscle group. This will help you become more aware of the difference. You should then continue to focus upon the muscle group for about 30 seconds during which time you present additional instructions to yourself to relax and enjoy the sensations of tension reduction. This will allow you to gradually learn to achieve greater relaxation. Self-instruction should be presented in a calm, confident slow, evenly paced manner. This same process of tension-release is repeated one or two more times or until you feel that th muscle group is very relaxed. Avoid instructions that assume a given state exists such as, "You are deeply relaxed," when it does not.

How to relax

Assume a comfortable position, preferably in an overstuffed chair with your arms resting on the arms of the chair. For greatest comfort, your legs can be extended, supported by a footrest. Your head should rest against some support and your eyes should be closed to allow you to concentrate more fully. All possible sources of distraction should be removed, such as ringing telephones and noisy people. If you feel pressed for time, it is best to wait until another time. You may practice relaxation right before going to sleep.

Learning to become relaxed is a skill and the aim of relaxation training is to attain this skill. An important aspect of such training is learning specific self-instructions which will help influence your anxiety. Taking a deep breath may be employed as one coping skill which you can practice during relaxation training. You might say to yourself: "Take a slow deep breath; very slowly fill your chest. (Pause) Now, exhale slowly (Pause) very slowly. (Pause) Note the changes in sensation as you gradually exhale."

The tension-release of each muscle group is repeated until you feel that the muscle group is relaxed. Only at this point would you progress to the tension-release of another muscle group. Try not to tense other muscles when you are practicing tension of one muscle group.

You should practice relaxation at home once or twice a day depending upon the time you have available. This practice consists of tensing and relaxing each muscle group, noting changes in sensation. Allow time at the end of the session to relax all muscles as much as possible. Practice the following relaxation sequence.

1. **Right hand and forearm**   Make a tight fist with your right hand and tense the muscles of your right forearm. (Pause) Hold this tension for about 5 to 7 seconds. Notice the sensation of tension in these muscles. Release all tension when you say the word "relax." Try to recognize the difference between tension and relaxation. Relaxing is an active movement.

Notice how these muscles feel as they become relaxed and allow 40 seconds to let these muscles relax further. Offer yourself suggestions for mental calmness as well as physical relaxation in a way that alters your state of tension. You might say: "I can deepen the relaxation by thinking silently to myself the words 'relax' and 'calm' as I let go. Just try to release more and more tension in these muscles. There's nothing else to be concerned about right now except relaxing and feeling comfortable. Just take a slow deep breath, and slowly exhale."

After giving yourself these instructions, check on your degree of relaxation of this muscle group. If it feels very relaxed, then continue to relax the muscles in your right hand and forearm as you now devote attention to the muscles in your upper right arm. If these muscles still feel somewhat tense, then repeat the process described above, trying to carry the relaxation further this time. Remember to notice the difference between relaxation and tension, and to use self-instructions to try to achieve a deeper level of relaxation. The sequence described above is repeated for each of the following muscle groups.

2. **Biceps of your right arm**   Keep your arm resting on the arm of your chair while you tense the muscles of your upper right arm.

3. **Hand and forearm of left arm**   Repeat procedure used for right arm.

4. **Biceps of left arm**   Repeat procedure used for biceps of right arm.

5. **Muscles in the forehead**   There are two major muscle groups in this region, one involved in frowning and the other involved when the forehead muscles are raised. To tense the former, frown as hard as you can; to tense the latter group, raise your forehead toward the ceiling as if you were surprised. Each should be practiced separately.

6. **Eye and nose muscles**   The eye muscles can be tensed by squinting your eyes tightly together. The muscles in your cheeks and upper lip can be tensed by wrinkling your nose. When these are tensed you should note changes in sensation in your upper lip and across your cheeks.

7. **Muscles in the lower part of the face**   These include the jaw muscles around your mouth, and they can be tensed by clenching your teeth together and pulling back the corners of your mouth. You should feel tension in the mouth muscles as well as in the muscles in front of your neck. Allow your teeth to part as you relax your jaw muscles.

8. **Neck muscles**   Your neck muscles can be tensed by pulling your chin downwards toward your chest while at the same time trying to prevent it from touching your chest.

9. **Chest, shoulders and upper back**   These muscles can be tensed by taking a deep breath and holding it, and, at the same time, pulling back the shoulder blades as if trying to make them touch. You should devote special attention to your thoracic muscles, those controlling respiration, since the respiratory rhythm can be used as an adjunct to relaxation. These muscles can be demonstrated by taking a very deep breath and then slowly exhaling, noticing that no effort is required while exhaling. This

should be repeated a few times until exhalation is perceived as letting go of muscle tension.

10. **Abdomen**   The abdominal muscles can be tensed by tightening up your stomach muscles, as if in anticipation of a hard punch in the stomach. These muscles can also be tensed by pulling them in tightly.

11. **Right upper leg**   Tense your upper right leg.

12. **Right calf and lower leg**   Pull your toes up toward your head.

13. **Right foot**   Push down with the toe and arch the foot. Do not tense these muscles very hard since a cramp may result.

14. **Left upper leg**   Repeat procedures used for right leg.

15. **Left calf and lower leg**   Repeat procedures used for right leg.

16. **Left foot**   Repeat procedures used for right foot.

Allow time at the end of each session to relax all muscles as far as possible, start from whatever point of relaxation exists. Be sure to determine whether you feel mentally calm as well as physically relaxed. If you do not feel any physical tension and feel calm inside, then you can end your practice session after taking a couple more minutes just to enjoy being relaxed and calm.

You can end practice sessions by counting from one to five during which time you tell yourself to slowly stretch your legs, move your hands and fingers, and move your head around. Counting can be done outloud or silently. You could end the session by giving yourself the following instructions: "I am now going to count to five and when I reach five, I will open my eyes and feel calm and refreshed. One (pause); two, I'll stretch my legs (pause); three, move my head around (pause); four, move my hands and fingers around (pause); five, open my eyes."

If you do not feel completely relaxed, go back over each muscle group, one at a time, and note whether tension is still present. When tension is found, offer yourself further relaxation instructions, or repeat the tension-release process. Your state of relaxation can then be reassessed. If you had trouble relaxing, try to identify what could have been added or avoided to enhance your relaxation.

A More Advanced Relaxation Procedure

Fewer steps are necessary as skill in relaxation is acquired. After tension can be perceived in a muscle group and you can release it, there is no further need to tense this group prior to relaxing it. You start from whatever point of relaxation already exists and then carry this as far as possible.

Bernstein and Borkovec* have developed a step-by-step procedure to move to a more abbreviated method. The criterion for progression is increasing skill in learning to relax tension, as well as increased discrimination of various states of tension. The advanced steps should not be employed until you have mastered earlier phases. And, you should not progress to the next muscle group until the prior one is fully relaxed. As with the procedure described above, time is allowed after each release to carry the relaxation further (about 30 seconds).

Procedures for seven muscle groups:
1. The muscles of your right arm are tensed and relaxed as a single group.
2. The same procedure is carried out for the muscles of your left arm.
3. All facial muscles are tensed at once.
4. Your neck muscle is tensed as described in the 16 group procedure.
5. Your chest, shoulder, upper back and abdomen muscles are tensed at once while taking and holding a deep breath.
6. The muscles of your right leg and foot are tensed by raising the leg slightly and tensing the upper leg, calf and foot.
7. The same procedure is followed for the left leg and foot.

Be sure to assess the level of relaxation attained after you go over these seven groups. Go over each group, and determine whether the muscles in this group are relaxed. If they are not, offer yourself additional self-instructions. It is best to move too slowly rather than too hastily.

When you can attain relaxed states using seven muscle groups, these can be reduced to four. Remember to include the breathing response as an adjunct to relaxation during these sessions.

Procedures for four muscle groups:
1. Both arms are tensed and released.
2. The face and neck muscles are tensed and released.
3. The chest, shoulders, back and abdomen are tensed and released.
4. Both legs are tensed and released.

Relaxation without prior tensing:
The same four muscle groups are employed, however, you do not deliberately tense your muscles. Instead, you focus on any tension that already exists in each group and offer yourself instructions to relax these muscles, recalling what it felt like when they were relaxed on other occasions.

The tension-release process can be reintroduced if you have trouble relaxing a particular muscle group.

Progress to a more advanced stage should not be made unless you have faithfully practiced earlier stages twice a day as recommended. These practice sessions are very important to learn discrimination of different states of tension and relaxation and for acquiring skill in learning to relax. People vary in the speed with which they become skilled in relaxing. Progress gradually after you have mastered each procedure.

Differential Relaxation

Differential relaxation consists of releasing unnecessary tension during daily activities. You do not tense your muscles but start from whatever state of relaxation already exists. Progressive relaxation training will help you to recognize the initial stages of tension as well as how to relax unnecessary tension. Relaxation can be induced by using the word you have said during practice, such as "calm" or "relax." This word will become a cue for you to relax.

There are other ways a cue word may be associated with a decrease in tension. For example, as Meichenbaum suggests, a word such as "relax" could be paired with slow deep breathing in which you take a series of slow deep breaths. When your chest is full, hold the air in for about five seconds and then gradually exhale, noting the changes in sensation as you do so and thinking about the word "relax." Gurman* has suggested another way to associate a cue word with a calm state. Here, you would practice relaxing at home while *vividly* describing outloud a pleasant relaxed scene. Select a cue word for this scene and practice twice daily, thinking about the scene after saying the cue word and achieving a relaxed state; you can use the cue word during the day when you start to feel anxious.

Feelings to Chart to Evaluate Progress

Number of times you caught yourself being relaxed with others.

Number of times you caught yourself being tense when with others.

Percentage of times you relaxed when you felt tense.

Sample Assignments

Practice relaxation twice a day for about 15 minutes over the next week.

Practice releasing unnecessary tension when you happen to remember to do so during the day.

Practice imagining a very pleasant situation and pairing this with a cue word such as "relax" twice a day.

Checklist

If you have difficulty learning to relax:

• You may progress to other muscle groups without making sure, through repeating tension and release cycles, that the muscles in one group are relaxed. It is better to progress slowly but surely than to go too fast.

- You may not be practicing frequently enough.

- You may be trying to practice when you feel rushed or when there are disturbing noises.

- Your anxiety may be related to thoughts and images rather than to muscle tension (see Chapter 14).

- You may not be able to discriminate between positive anticipations and discomfort.

- You may have difficulty keeping intrusive thoughts out of your mind when trying to relax. Use a more continual stream of relaxing suggestions.

- Occasionally difficulty in relaxing occurs due to fear of "letting go." Keep in mind that relaxation training is a skill which *you* employ to influence your tension.

- You may experience such a persistent state of tension that any drop in this appears to be a very relaxed state. If this is true it may take you longer than usual in terms of number of practice sessions to learn to identify differing degrees of tension and to obtain a calm relaxed state.

- You may have trouble identifying tension. Keep a daily log of any changes you notice in anxiety and write down very specifically what you feel at these times. Include notation of the location of any muscle tension as well as other sensations you experience, such as rapid heartbeat, perspiring, flushing, increases in breathing rate, butterflies in your stomach, nausea or dry mouth.

- Perhaps you are not employing your new skills to decrease tension during the day. The more you practice, the more effective these skills will become.

*see Bibliography and References

16

Issues of Special Concern to Women

As a female reader, you may be asking, "Will being more assertive in initiating social contacts result in my being perceived by others as 'pushy' and 'unfeminine'?" This may be a realistic concern; however, it is important that you compare the possible consequences of being active in making social contacts to the consequences of being retiring or remaining passive.

The social role expectations for women have typically prescribed that women be the receiver of initiations from men, let men make the decisions to terminate or extend contacts, allow men to decide which subjects to bring up and which to pursue, and so on. However, the stereotypes of what are appropriate behaviors for women and men in social encounters are rapidly undergoing alteration. More and more women are questioning the desirability of traditional sex roles. Many women are realizing that they want to, and are often being asked to, "carry their own weight" in both the economic and social arenas. However, there are few "skill laboratories" where women can learn the necessary social skills which go along with increased independence and autonomy. Many women find that they are not equipped to develop a new social network after being divorced or widowed. For all women, the choice is clear: become socially visible, take the initiative in making contacts and risk occasionally negative reactions, or remain passive and isolated and risk loneliness and boredom. With either alternative, there are costs and benefits involved. It is our belief that choosing to become an active participant in life will result in greater payoffs than the risks and disappointments that you may experience. It is likely that you have already made a choice between these options. Deciding to take the time and energy to build your social skills by working with this book indicates that you have chosen to be active rather than passive.

Anticipating a Negative Response

It is important to consider how you will handle adverse reactions to

141

your social assertions if these occur. Often however, the negative consequences that women expect to follow their assertions never
materialize. In fact, it has been our experience, that the reactions of
others are often neutral or surprisingly positive. Try not to inhibit your
initiations or allow yourself to feel anxious because you *anticipate* a
negative response. Remind yourself that women often use self- cen-
sorship to protect themselves from imagined adverse reactions. The
best way to test out your fantasies is to take the initiative and see what
happens.

Attempting *small* risks at first will help you overcome your hesitation. There will be occasions when the reactions of others may be less
than what you hoped for. Behaviors which may be seen as appropriately assertive when displayed by a man, may still be labeled by some
people as "aggressive" and inappropriate when displayed by a woman
(such as initiating a conversation with a stranger or resisting interruption). There may be situations when your behavior was well timed and
skillfully executed, but you still receive an unsatisfactory response. In
these instances, the problem may be with the other person. He may not
feel comfortable interacting with a woman on an equal basis, or his
masculine image may require him to always be the "dominant" person,
the decision-maker, the "boss." Fortunately, more and more men are
abandoning the "macho" image with its overabundance of pressures
and responsibilities, and choosing instead a pattern of sharing and
compromise when it comes to interacting with women. If you do get a
negative reaction from someone who does not embrace the idea of
male-female equality, then you need to look elsewhere for support for
your social assertiveness, otherwise, your new skills may deteriorate.

Using Self-Praise as Reinforcement

Since positive reactions from others are not guaranteed, it is important
that women learn to praise themselves for their own assertions. Self-
approval for initiating a conversation, disagreeing, or terminating an
exchange can increase the likelihood that you will attempt these
behaviors again, even if you experience a negative response from
others. It is especially important for women to use self-praise, not only
because it can take the place of positive social consequences, but also
because women seem to congratulate themselves less than men for their
own accomplishments.

In addition to using self-reinforcement as a means to counteract
the occasional social "costs" of taking the initiative, it is also important
that women identify existing sources of social approval as well as
develop new sources. You may find it helpful to use a friend as a source
of praise for your new skills. You could tell your friend that you need

some positive feedback for your attempts, especially when the outcome is not what you had hoped for. You may want to ask your friend to accompany you during some of your weekly assignments to provide support as well as immediate praise and corrective feedback. You may also wish to seek out additional sources of social support. Many women find the encouragement they need to make important changes in their lives by joining a rap group or consciousness-raising group.

Keeping the Context in Mind

Another consideration in reducing the probability of adverse consequences is to modify your approach in certain situations. Women may have to be more sensitive than men to the appropriateness of taking the initiative in certain circumstances. For example, the timing of your initiation, the kinds of behavior you display (smiles, eye contact, being near), and the content of your opening remark may all need to be carefully considered. For instance, you may find that in more formal settings or with men who are more "traditional," you are more likely to get positive responses from the men if you ask for assistance or advice than if you make a personal observation about the person. Since women are often expected to be pleasant, friendly, and compassionate most of the time, upsetting this expectation by disagreeing, giving negative feedback, or resisting interruption could have negative consequences. It may be especially important for women to be courteous and tactful in their interactions, especially in the beginning when new assertive skills may come as a surprise to acquaintances and friends.

In addition to reducing the likelihood of negative consequences by modifying your approach to situations and lessening the impact of unpleasant responses by utilizing other sources of reinforcement, it is also important that you have the skills to handle negative reactions from others when they do occur.

How to Handle Putdowns

There may be occasions when women are confronted with sexist remarks and putdowns. It is reassuring to know that if a rude or embarrassing comment is made, you have some idea of how to handle the situation. One important thing to remember is not to merely laugh it off, or smile your discomfort away. For many women, a smile is like a reflex action in embarrassing or anger-provoking situations. Take time to respond in your own way. Do not feel pressured to react immediately. You may have to practice not smiling in such situations, since this is so habitual for many women. By not displaying a smile of appreciation, the other person gets the message that their remark was not funny to you. You may wish to say, "I don't think that was funny." If the person responds with, "What's the matter, honey, no sense of humor?" you could repeat your initial comment without getting into a prolonged discussion or defense of your reaction.

You may also find it helpful to have a few "stock" responses that can be used in a variety of situations. Some suggested by Fensterheim and Baer* are:

"I feel demeaned by that remark."
"Oh, come on now, that's really in poor taste."
"That sounds like a putdown to me."
"That's a very hostile comment."
"Why are you so uptight about this?"

As more women effectively handle negative reactions from others, such responses will occur less often. Also, as more women take the initiative in social relationships, the social expectations of what is appropriately "feminine" will alter and expand. As more and more women become assertive in their behavior, the patterns of female passivity will break down. Sex roles are being challenged today, and the changes will undoubtedly benefit both men and women.

*see Bibliography and References

17

The Use of Groups for Social Skill Training

This book can be used in groups specially arranged for purposes of social skill training or in already formed groups such as women's rap groups, single parent groups, and groups for the divorced, where the book could be employed as part of ongoing programs for self- enhancement.

There are some advantages to pursuing your individual program with others who have similar goals. A group provides many opportunities to rehearse skills and this practice can provide an intermediate step to "real" social situations. It also provides many opportunities for feedback, suggestions, model presentation, and support from others. It is sometimes difficult to rely totally on your own evaluation and reinforcement of your skills and your attempts to be more socially active. A group can provide you with partners to share assignments. Perhaps the most difficult aspect of trying to change your own behavior, even when the outcome is desirable, is *consistently* carrying out the steps necessary. The agreement to report back to the group each week concerning your progress may help you to complete chosen assignments. A group offers others with whom you may form a verbal or written agreement to help complete assignments. These "contracts" should identify the exact tasks to be completed, for example, you may agree to initiate two conversations with strangers during the next week and the other person may agree to offer two elaborated opinion statements during her weekly staff meeting. The consequences for completion of, or failure to perform tasks should be explicitly described. For example, you may each contribute three dollars and go see a movie together if each of you completes your assignments. Whoever does not complete her assignment must put in another three dollars and take the other person to a movie, and, if neither of you complete your assignment, you may agree to each send three dollars to your least favorite charity. The particular rewards, costs and tasks involved should be individually tailored for each person. A reasonable size for such a group, is between five and twelve members. Meetings could be held once a week for a two-hour period. For further guidelines on group structure and process see Chapter 4 in Osborn and Harris.

How to Use this Book

The suggestions offered below provide a rudimentary outline of how a group might utilize this book chapter by chapter. Of course, the number of possibilities in terms of group structure and content is limited only by your own imagination and energy.

After everyone has read and discussed the *Introduction* and *Chapter 1, Chapter 2* could be the subject of another group session. Individual goals could be discussed and established for each person. The first assignment could be for each person to observe his social behavior during the next week and to collect information relevant to his desired goals using the guidelines described in Chapter 2.

Practicing new behavior and selecting assignments Information collected should be reviewed at the beginning of the third session and *Chapters 3* and *4* reviewed where suggestions are offered on what to do differently, for rehearsing behaviors and for selecting assignments. This session should permit practice of new behaviors and offering of models, feedback and suggestions to each participant concerning their selected behaviors. Group members could also select and practice assignments they have agreed to try out during the following week with other group members volunteering to play needed roles. Each person's progress should be compared with her *own* unique skill and comfort levels, and support and praise offered for achievements in relation to this. The emphasis is upon offering *constructive* feedback in which improvements are reinforced and critical comments such as, "You can do better," are avoided. The more specific the feedback, the more helpful it is, because the person can more accurately identify what s(he) should do differently. Someone practicing how to initiate conversations could be informed, "Your eye contact was great that time and you smiled."

Only one or two behaviors may be practiced during a session depending upon skill and comfort levels. Let us say that Mrs. L. wishes to increase her skills in initiating conversations and during a role-play carried out for assessment purposes, the group notices that she does not look at her partner or smile, and speaks with a very flat tone of voice. During feedback, the group would first point out any positive aspects of her verbal or nonverbal behavior and then offer suggestions on what she might change for the better. For example, one group member might observe: "What you said to her was really very good. It related to the situation at hand and you told her something about yourself. (Notice she says *why* it was good.) Perhaps if you smiled when you said this, looked at her more often and used a more lively tone of voice, she would be even more interested in pursuing the exchange." During rehearsal, Mrs. L. may concentrate upon smiling more and increasing her eye contact, and at the next session work on a more lively intonation. Other group members could model a "more lively tone of voice" for her.

From the third session, each participant may move at a somewhat different rate. Some members will have identified and practiced necessary behaviors and be ready to try out their first assignment. Others may feel they need to gather more information on how to change their behavior and decide that during the next week they will observe others to try to define what it is they should do differently. Each person should select an assignment related to accomplishment of her desired objectives each week. Also, each participant should decide how to evaluate his or her progress. Part of a session can be devoted to discussing the importance of finding out what is happening by drawing from the material in *Chapter 6*.

A discussion of each person's past week's assignment should be held first at each meeting. This highlights the importance of carrying out assignments. Progress reports, including presentation of data and identification of next steps to be pursued, should be discussed at each session. These may reveal that skills were underestimated or overestimated.

Developing self-reinforcement   To encourage the development of self-reinforcement as discussed in *Chapter 5*, the group could ask each member to praise their accomplishments outloud at first and make group feedback contingent on this self-praise. When members rehearse situations within sessions or report activities from the past week, each should evaluate his or her own performance first and praise any improvement or success, regardless of how "minor," before the other members give their feedback, suggestions and recognition. In this way, members have to "earn" the feedback and support of the group by first taking the responsibility of evaluating and supporting their own efforts. The group should establish a "rule" whereby any general self-criticism is discouraged and only self-praise and specific suggestions for improvement are acceptable. In this way, the group encourages self- reinforcement and specific problem-solving attempts and discourages "failure talk" and feelings of hopelessness.

Where to go to meet others   In determining where to go to meet people (*Chapter 7*), the group session could include a discussion of the members' interests and situations in which they have and have not been successful in meeting people. Members could also agree to go together, either in pairs or small groups, to several events during the weeks to come—for example, on an outing with a hiking club, a singles' party, or a lecture, and observe each other occasionally as attempts are made to initiate conversations in these situations. Each can then benefit from feedback based on such observations.

Learning conversational skills   When covering *Chapter 8* on methods of initiating conversations, the group session could become a "laboratory" in which members practice various initiating strategies with each other. Initial exercises could require that others react to initiations in a positive manner while later attempts could be met with more neutral and negative reactions. In this way, group members can rehearse how they would react to a variety of responses from others. The group could also simulate a party situation or other group gathering where specific "target" persons would have the task of initiating conversations with individuals or joining small group discussions.

Maintaining conversations could be practiced by having members break into small groups and attempt to change the purpose and content of the conversation with various reactions from the other participants. Practice exercises as discussed in *Chapter 9* could also require each group member to come prepared to discuss two topics in detail or to tell a story or incident about oneself to a small group. Creating a more personal exchange could also be practiced.

When covering *Chapter 10*, members could practice terminating conversations with each other as well as arranging future or continued contacts either face to face or over the telephone. Various ways to handle enthusiastic, cool, or rejecting reactions could be demonstrated and practiced including the use of positive self-instructions.

To practice changing your participation in conversations (*Chapter 11*), small groups of three or four persons could be formed, some topic selected, and the tasks of each group might include using elaborated opinion statements, breaking into an ongoing conversation without interrupting it, and attempting to resist interruptions. If some members have trouble monopolizing conversations, they could practice asking others for their points of view.

When discussing how to have more enjoyable conversations, the group members could practice giving positive feedback to each other using a variety of reinforcing words and phrases. Each person could be requested to bring in two reinforcing words or phrases not contained in *Chapter 12* and these could be shared with the group and lisited for future reference. Being a good listener could be practiced by using groups of three in which the role of one person is to display "listening skills" and the role of the other two is to offer feedback after a brief discussion is held.

Learning to disagree   To practice disagreeing with others, the members could choose a controversial topic and divide the group in half, one side taking one stand, the other side taking the opposite position. Each person could then offer at least one comment in support of their side's positon (regardless of the individuals' "real" beliefs). Thus, each member would be given a chance to practice offering a difference of opinion while observing how others handle disagreement. This discussion could terminate with a general summation of the comments which were especially good and worth remembering for practice in real discussions. To practice expressing negative feelings each person could role-play a situation in which they would like to express negative feelings with the help of other members who act out the part of involved others. It may first be necessary to obtain a description of how these others usually act so that whoever plays the part of the involved party will respond realistically. Support and suggestions of other ways to handle the situation can then be offered and new behaviors practiced.

Learning to use positive self-instructions   The group could help each member develop and use positive self-instructions by identifying negative thoughts and their destructive effects and developing workable positive counterparts. Some group members could be asked to select a specific social situation in which they feel uncomfortable and to share with the others what goes through their minds, their thoughts and images, in this situation. Other group members could be requested to select some specific social situation in which they perform very well and share the thoughts and images they have in this situation. This should serve to identify specific types of negative and positive self-statements   and to highlight the relationship of the kinds of thoughts one has (negative or positive) to performance and comfort in social situations. The group members can also provide useful input in terms of examining the rationality of negative thoughts, and the implications even if the statements are true. Members could also assist each other by sharing their successful strategies for overcoming negative thoughts.

Learning to relax   Relaxation could be practiced during sessions using taped instructions. Individual difficulties in achieving a state of relaxation could be discussed and various suggestions for relieving tension offered. Members could also share their efforts to practice relaxation at home and in social situations.

Follow-up sessions   To maintain change over time, the group could agree to have periodic follow-up or booster sessions to share progress reports and offer support and direction for further change. If meetings are not possible, then the group may encourage periodic phone calls among members to provide some continuing contact.

18

Next Steps

Often, the rewards attained from new social skills by obtaining more positive feedback from others, having more freedom to initiate contacts, and being more successful in your attempts, will be sufficient to insure the continued use of your new skills. You may come to take new changes "for granted" and expect these to persist without continuing efforts on your part. You may gradually forget to use self-reinforcement and set assignments to maintain your progress. You could, however, have an ongoing agreement with yourself, that each week you will initiate two conversations with strangers. This will insure that you maintain your skills in this area while exposing you to interaction with new people each week. Such agreements also provide for practicing more innovative and "risky" social behaviors. Self-reinforcement is especially important in the maintenance of social behavior as there is always the risk that you will be turned down when you try to arrange a future contact or ignored when you try to initiate a conversation.

It may be helpful to arrange support from another person who may also be interested in maintaining new social behaviors. You could meet every other week for an hour or so and share any new skills that you have tried.

There is another sense in which we may "take things for granted" and this refers to becoming accustomed to new changes so that they no longer seem as positive or exciting. It may seem to you that even though you are having more frequent social contacts they no longer provide the pleasure they did in the past. The first constructive task you could carry out, if this applies to you, is to monitor your behavior for a week and see if this matches your estimate of where things are. Let us say that your goal was to have six social contacts each week which lasted between one and five hours, and now feel that even though you are having these, you no longer like them as much. Monitoring your behavior may indicate that, in fact, you have not maintained this level. Thus, dissatisfaction with aspects of the social behavior you have tried to change should be a cue for you to collect some information to make sure that you have achieved your goals. If you have not, then you could review specific chapters as needed and select appropriate assignments.

What if this information indicates that you are indeed having six social contacts of this duration per week? You can scan these to make sure they meet other criterion you have set for yourself for such meetings. Were these contacts with people you selected as your target group? The data you collect will inform you whether you have deviated from desired objectives in ways that are important to your satisfaction. If the data you collect indicates that you are having as many social contacts as you set for yourself, then try to identify what you could change to heighten your satisfaction. You may be ready to move on to more challenging goals.

Taking More Risks

As you become comfortable and are successful with new behaviors, you may wish to try out ones which entail more of a risk—for example, the possibility of rejection. In the past, the very thought of rejection might have been crushing to you. Now, self-reinforcement hopefully plays a more important role and you can more realistically evaluate the implications of various consequences so that rejection is not the end of the world. As the imagined risks entailed in initiating social contacts are placed in more realistic perspective, you may feel free to try out new variations of social behaviors. You may be ready to "try again" when met with a minimal reply or when turned down for a meeting or date.

Extending Yourself

You may also find that, as you become more comfortable in social situations, you are more willing and able to offer positive cues, such as smiles and eye contact, to others even though they do not take the initiative in offering these to you. You may find that now when you walk down the street, rather than avoiding eye contact with others and never smiling at someone unless they smile at you first, you now seek eye contact and take the initiative in smiling. You may also find that you take the initiative in greeting people more frequently. The less you "catastrophize" possible rejection, and the more you reinforce yourself for extending yourself despite the consequences, the more you will be willing to extend yourself in this manner.

You may also be more willing and able to offer positive replies in response to negative statements by others. Gains may spread from one area to another. For example, your ability to be positive in response to negative responses in social interactions with friends and acquaintances may help you when you have difficulty in service situations. If a clerk is "short" with you, rather than snapping at him you might say, "It looks like you've had a hard day." That is, you may be able to use "empathic responses" more frequently.

Changing your behavior in the ways described in this book involves you in self-management of your own behavior. Such management requires many skills—such as being able to identify needed changes, selecting useful assignments, carrying these out, and offering yourself reinforcement. Some of us have had more experience with self-management. Certainly one of the most difficult aspects is getting yourself to carry out agreed-upon assignments. Even though this manual has provided guidelines which will help you avoid many of the reasons why such resolutions fail, you may need the support of a group and/or a counselor to help you to alter your behavior.

You may now be ready to move on to new levels in terms of developing continuing relationships. Although many of the skills discussed in this book will make this easier, you may need to develop additional skills to maintain such lasting relationships, such as learning to "negotiate" behavior exchanges with significant others.

Information to Evaluate Your Progress

- Figure the percentage of your exchanges where you made the other person laugh.
- Figure the percentage of times you found yourself really interested in what another person was saying.
- Find the rate of compliments you offer others.

Checklist

If you are not having enjoyable conversations:

- Perhaps you expect your conversations to be enjoyable without any effort on your part?
- Perhaps you do not listen to what others say.
- Perhaps you engage in too much negative talk.
- You may not "personalize" the content enough. Perhaps you have shown no interest in someone by reinforcing her for specific things that she does that you like and asking appropriate personal questions. Or perhaps you do not share enough information about yourself.
- You may allow yourself to be manipulated into talking about things you don't want to or become defensive. You may need to practice saying no and responding nondefensively to accusatory remarks.
- You may have irrational beliefs which interfere with your enjoyment of social exchanges and should re-evaluate these.
- Are you interested in offering the other person an enjoyable experience as well as yourself?
- You may be going overboard with a behavior, that is, smiling too frequently or looking so long that others become uncomfortable.
- You may not have increased the frequency of a positive behavior enough. Instead of not smiling at all during your exchanges, you may now smile once every thirty minutes. Try to be more generous.
- Perhaps you increased your positive behaviors but forgot to decrease negative ones. Perhaps you are now smiling as you frown so that the latter dilutes the effect of your smiles.

APPENDIX A

Checklist A
Assessing Social Contacts

WEEK OF _____

*S/A: S=Stranger; A=Acquaintance (someone slightly familiar or a friend)
**Other's response: + =positive; 0=neutral; -=negative
***Enjoyment: 1=not at all; 2=a little; 3=a fair amount; 4=much; 5=very much

#	Date & day of week	Sex (M/F) Age	S/A*	Place & Time	Did you initiate? Yes/No	If you initiated, what did you say?	Other's response (+, 0, -)**	Duration (min.)	Enjoy-ment (1-5)***
1									
2.									
3.									
4.									
5.									
6.									
7.									
8.									
9.									
10.									
11.									
12.									
13.									

Side One

Situations where I could have started a conversation but did not

Date	Place	Sex	Circumstances

Side Two

APPENDIX B

Situation Summary Sheet

To be used to summarize information obtained
from weekly checklist A.

Week	Situations			
	1. _____	5. _____		
	2. _____	6. _____		
	3. _____	7. _____		
	4. _____	8. _____		
	1. _____	5. _____		
	2. _____	6. _____		
	3. _____	7. _____		
	4. _____	8. _____		
	1. _____	5. _____		
	2. _____	6. _____		
	3. _____	7. _____		
	4. _____	8. _____		
	1. _____	5. _____		
	2. _____	6. _____		
	3. _____	7. _____		
	4. _____	8. _____		
	1. _____	5. _____		
	2. _____	6. _____		
	3. _____	7. _____		
	4. _____	8. _____		
	1. _____	5. _____		
	2. _____	6. _____		
	3. _____	7. _____		
	4. _____	8. _____		

Checklist B
Identifying Behavior

Fill out one checklist for each extended conversation which was particularly pleasant or unpleasant as listed on Checklist (A).

WEEK OF _____ **# from Checklist (A)** _____

For each item, check the appropriate box that describes your behavior, thought, or feeling:

ITEM	not at all (1)	a little (2)	about half the time (3)	most of the time (4)	all of the time (5)
Positive 1. I contributed my share of talk to the conversation.					
2. I expressed positive feelings and opinions when I felt like it.					
3. I disagreed when I felt like it.					
4. I initiated some topics of conversation.					
5. I smiled and showed interest in the other person.					
6. The conversation was interesting.					
Negative 7. I worried that I would bore the person.					
8. I felt tense and nervous.					
9. I worried that I would run out of things to say.					

10. Future contract arranged?   Yes _____   No _____

NOTE: Please turn sheet over and answer items.

ADDITIONAL COMMENTS:

1. Interesting, pleasant things you noticed about the other person:

    a.

    b.

    c.

2. Reservations you had about the other person; things that bothered you:

    a.

    b.

    c.

3. Strengths in your own performance; things you did or said well:

    a.

    b.

    c.

4. Specific behaviors, thoughts or feelings that were troublesome and that you would like to increase or decrease:

What you do now	*What you would like to do*
a.	a.
b.	b.
c.	c.
d.	d.

Assertion Inventory

Many people experience difficulty in handling interpersonal situations requiring them to assert themselves in some way, for example, turning down a request or asking a favor. Please indicate your degree of discomfort or anxiety in the space provided *before* each situation listed below. Use the following scale to indicate degree of discomfort:

1 = none / 2 = a little / 3 = a fair amount / 4 = much /
5 = very much

Then, go over the list a second time and indicate *after* each item the probability or likelihood of your displaying the behavior if actually presented with the situation.* For example, if you rarely apologize when you are at fault, you would mark "4" after that item. Use the following scale to indicate response probability:

1 = always do it / 2 = usually do it / 3 = do it about half the time
4 = rarely do it / 5 = never do it

*NOTE:

It is important to assess your discomfort ratings apart from your response probability. Otherwise, one may contaminate the other. To prevent this, place a piece of paper over your discomfort ratings while responding to the situations a second time for your response probability.

Degree of Dis- comfort	SITUATION	Response Prob- ability
_____	1. Turn down a request to borrow your car	_____
_____	2. Compliment a friend	_____
_____	3. Ask a favor of someone	_____
_____	4. Resist sales pressure.	_____
_____	5. Apologize when you are at fault	_____
_____	6. Turn down a request for a meeting or date	_____
_____	7. Admit fear and request consideration	_____
_____	8. Tell a person you are intimately involved with when he/she says or does something that bothers you	_____
_____	9. Ask for a raise	_____
_____	10. Admit ignorance in some area	_____
_____	11. Turn down a request to borrow money . . .	_____
_____	12. Ask personal questions	_____
_____	13. Turn off a talkative friend	_____

_____ 14. Ask for constructive criticism . . . . _____
_____ 15. Initiate a conversation with a stranger . . . . _____
16. Compliment a person you are romantically
_____   involved with or interested in . . . . _____
_____ 17. Request a meeting or a date with a person . _____
18. Your initial request for a meeting is turned
       down and you ask the person again at a
_____   later time. . . . . _____
19. Admit confusion about a point under
_____   discussion and ask for clarification . . . . . . _____
_____ 20. Apply for a job . . . . _____
_____ 21. Ask whether you have offended someone . _____
_____ 22. Tell someone that you like them . . . . _____
23. Request expected service when such is not
_____   forthcoming, e.g., in a restaurant . . . . _____
24. Discuss openly with the person his/her
_____   criticism of your behavior . . . . _____
25. Return defective items, e.g., store or
_____   restaurant . . . . _____
26. Express an opinion that differs from that of
_____   the person you are talking to . . . . _____
27. Resist sexual overtures when you are not
_____   interested. . . . . _____
28. Tell the person when you feel he/she has
_____   done something that is unfair to you . . . . . _____
_____ 29. Accept a date. . . . . _____
_____ 30. Tell someone good news about yourself. . . _____
_____ 31. Resist pressure to drink . . . . _____
_____ 32. Resist a significant person's unfair demand _____
_____ 33. Quit a job . . . . _____
_____ 34. Resist pressure to "turn on" . . . . _____
35. Discuss openly with a person his/her
_____   criticism of your work. . . . . _____
_____ 36. Request the return of borrowed items . . . . _____
_____ 37. Receive compliments . . . . _____
38. Continue to converse with someone who
_____   disagrees with you. . . . . _____
39. Tell a friend or someone with whom you
       work when he/she says or does something
_____   that bothers you . . . . _____
40. Ask a person who is annoying you in a
_____   public situation to stop . . . . _____

Please indicate the situations you would like to handle more assertively by placing a circle around the item number.

APPENDIX E

Weekly Social Contacts Sheet

Goal: _____

Week	AEL*	Total #	# with strangers	Length of contacts in minutes						# with acquaintances	Length of contact in minutes					
				3'-5'	6'-15'	16'-30'	31'-60'	61'-120'	Over		3'-5'	6'-15'	16'-30'	31'-60'	61'-120'	Over
		M	___M( )**							___M( )***						
		F	F( )							F( )						
		M	___M( )**							___M( )***						
		F	F( )							F( )						
		M	___M( )**							___M( )***						
		F	F( )							F( )						
		M	___M( )**							___M( )***						
		F	F( )							F( )						
		M	___M( )**							___M( )***						
		F	F( )							F( )						
		M	___M( )**							___M( )***						
		F	F( )							F( )						
		M	___M( )**							___M( )***						
		F	F( )							F( )						

* AEL = Average enjoyment level (Total Checklist A figures separately by males and females and divide by number of each)
** In parentheses, insert how many of these you initiated
*** Number of different people

APPENDIX F
Script Cards

Situation:

What you say:

Response:

What you say:

Situation:

What you say:

Response:

What you say:

Situation:

What s(he) says

What you say:

What s(he) says:

What you say:

APPENDIX G
Behavior Assignment Sheet

No.	Date	Assignment	Date Completed
1.			
2.			
3.			
4.			
5.			
6.			
7.			
8.			
9.			
10.			
11.			
12.			
13.			
14.			
15.			
16.			

Recording Form For Frequency Count

	Time		Total	No. of	Daily
Date	Start	Stop	Time	Behaviors	Rate

Name: _____   Date: _____

Behavior: _____

	Time		Total	No. of	Daily
Date	Start	Stop	Time	Behaviors	Rate

Recording Form for Percentage Measure

Name: _____   Date: _____

Behavior: _____   Daily Percent: _____

Times Checked	Behavior yes/no	Time Checked	Behavior yes/no
1.		11.	
2.		12.	
3.		13.	
4.		14.	
5.		15.	
6.		16.	
7.		17.	
8.		18.	
9.		19.	
10.		20.	

APPENDIX J

Blank Chart

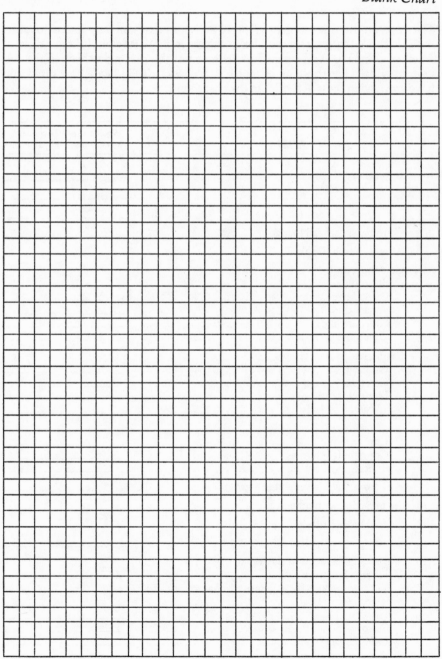

Activity Inventory

The items on this questionnaire refer to activities that you may find enjoyable. Indicate those that you would like to engage in more frequently, regardless of whether you have ever engaged in them or not, by placing a check in the column provided. For those items which you check, also indicate how often you have engaged in these activities in the past month.

Activity	Would like to do more often	Frequency in the past month
1. Visit others...........................	_____	_____
2. Go to parties...........................	_____	_____
3. Participate in informal get-togethers for coffee/drink	_____	_____
4. Go to bars, cocktail lounges	_____	_____
5. Attend church socials	_____	_____
6. Go dancing:		
Ballroom...............................	_____	_____
Discotheque.............................	_____	_____
Square dancing	_____	_____
Folk dancing	_____	_____
Other(s) (specify)........................	_____	_____
7. Participate in craft classes:		
Painting...............................	_____	_____
Ceramics...............................	_____	_____
Photography	_____	_____
Other (s) (specify)	_____	_____
8. Sing in a group:		
Church choir	_____	_____
Community chorus	_____	_____
Other(s) (specify)........................	_____	_____
9. Play a musical instrument in a group	_____	_____
10. Go bicycling with others......................	_____	_____
11. Go hiking with others........................	_____	_____
12. Go camping with others	_____	_____
13. Attend adult education classes:		
Foreign language	_____	_____
Technical skills (e.g. auto mechanics, drafting, accounting)	_____	_____
History	_____	_____
Science	_____	_____
Other(s) (specify).......................	_____	_____
14. Play games:		
Cards (specify).........................	_____	_____

Chess/checkers .... _____ _____
Scrabble .... _____ _____
Other(s) (specify)......................... _____ _____

15. Engage in group volunteer work, fund raising, community projects, etc., (specify)............. _____ _____

16. Attend hobbie clubs/organizations:
Photography .... _____ _____
Gardening .... _____ _____
Antiques .... _____ _____
Travel .... _____ _____
Other(s) (specify)......................... _____ _____

17. Participate in sports:
Baseball................................. _____ _____
Tennis .... _____ _____
Golf..................................... _____ _____
Swimming................................ _____ _____
Pool/billiards .... _____ _____
Judo/karate............................. _____ _____
Bowling................................. _____ _____
Skiing .... _____ _____
Volleyball .... _____ _____
Horseback riding......................... _____ _____
Motorcycling............................. _____ _____
Table tennis (ping pong) .... _____ _____
Other(s) (specify)......................... _____ _____

18. Attend meetings of special interest groups:
Ecology .... _____ _____
Travel .... _____ _____
PTA .... _____ _____
Bridge club .... _____ _____
Political group........................... _____ _____
Other(s) (specify)......................... _____ _____

19. Go to movies:
Stage plays .... _____ _____
Travel films............................. _____ _____
Concerts .... _____ _____
Operas.................................. _____ _____
Ballets .... _____ _____

20. Attend lectures:
Science .... _____ _____
Travel .... _____ _____
Politics .... _____ _____
Other(s) (specify)......................... _____ _____

21. Visit museums:
Art .... _____ _____
History .... _____ _____
Science .... _____ _____

22. Attend exhibits or shows:
Flowers .... _____ _____
Automobiles .... _____ _____

Boats.................................... _____ _____
Arts and crafts.......................... _____ _____
Animal shows .... _____ _____
Other(s) (specify)....................... _____ _____

23. Look at:
    Interesting buildings .... _____ _____
    Beautiful scenery .... _____ _____
    Other people .... _____ _____

24. Go to the zoo .... _____ _____

25. Visit new places:
    Parks.................................... _____ _____
    Neighborhoods .... _____ _____
    Towns .... _____ _____
    Historical landmarks...................... _____ _____
    Restaurants .... _____ _____
    Other(s) (specify)....................... _____ _____

26. Go to coffee houses....................... _____ _____

27. Go to sport events .... _____ _____

28. Take a walk .... _____ _____

29. Go shopping.............................. _____ _____

30. Visit libraries .... _____ _____

31. Invite people over........................ _____ _____

32. Other activities not mentioned (specify) .... _____ _____

Bibliography and References

Those of special interest are marked*.

*Alberti, R. E. and Emmons, M.L. *Your Perfect Right*. San Luis Obispo: Impact Press, 1974.

Bach, G. R. and Deutsch, R. M. *Pairing*. New York: Wyden, 1970.

Bach, G.R. and Wyden, P. *The Intimate Enemy*. New York: William Morrow, 1969.

*Bernstein, D. A. and Borkovec, J. D. *Progressive Relaxation Training: A Manual for the Helping Professions*. Champaign: Research Press, 1973.

Christensen, A., Arkowitz, H. and Anderson, J. "Practice dating as treatment for college dating inhibitions." *Behaviour Research and Therapy*, 13, 1975, pp. 321–331.

Correctional Officer Training Program. Rehabilitation Research Foundation, P. O. Box 3587, Montgomery, AL 36109.

Eisler, R. M., Miller, P. M. and Hersen, M. "Components of assertive behavior." *Journal of Clinical Psychology*, 29, 1973, pp. 295–299.

Eisler, R. M. Hersen, M., Miller, P. M. and Blanchard, E. B. "Situational determinants of assertive behavior." *Journal of Consulting and Clinical Psychology*, 43, 1973, pp. 330–340.

Ellis, A. *Reason and Emotion in Psychotherapy*. New York: Stuart, 1962.

*Fensterheim, H. and Baer, J. *Don't Say Yes When You Want to Say No*. New York: Dell, 1975.

Fisher, J. D. and Byrne, D. "Too close for comfort: Sex differences in response to invasions of personal space." *Journal of Personality and Social Psychology*, 32, 1975, pp. 15–21.

Gambrill, E. D. "It's up to you: Assertive training for women." Videotape prepared for presentation at the Seventh Annual Conference in Behavior Modification. Banff, Canada, 1975.

Gambrill, E. D. and Richey, C. A. "An assertion inventory for use in assessment and research." *Behavior Therapy*, 6, 1975, pp. 550–561.

Gambrill, E. D. "A behavioral program for increasing social interaction." Paper presented at the Seventh Annual Convention of the Association for Advancement of Behavior Therapy, Miami Beach, December 1973.

Glass, C. "Response acquisition and cognitive self-statement modification approaches to dating behavior training." Doctoral dissertation, Indiana University, 1974.

Goldfried, M., Decenteceo, E. T. and Weinberg, L. "Systematic rational restructuring as a self-control technique." *Behavior Therapy* 5, 1974, pp. 247–254.

Goldsmith, J. B. and McFall, R. M. "Development and evaluation of an interpersonal skills training program for psychiatric patients." *Journal of Abnormal Psychology*, 84, 1975, pp. 51–58.

Gurman, A. S. "Treatment of a case of public speaking anxiety by *in vivo* desensitization and cue controlled relaxation." *Journal of Behavior Therapy and Experimental Psychiatry*, 4, 1973, pp. 51–54.

Homme, L. and Addison, R. "The reinforcing event (RE) menu." *NSPI Journal*, 1, 1966, pp. 8–9.

Kanfer, F. H. "The maintenance of behavior by self-generated stimuli and reinforcement." In *The Psychology of Private Events: Perspective on Covert Response Systems*. A. Jacobs and L. Sachs (eds). New York: Academic Press, 1971, pp. 39–59.

Kazdin, A. E. "Effects of covert modeling and model reinforcement on assertive behavior." Journal of Abnormal Psychology 83, 1974, pp. 240–252.

Kazdin, A. E. "Self-monitoring and behavior change." In J. Mahoney and C. E. Thorensen, *Self-control: Power to the Person*. Monterey: Brooks/Cole, 1974.

Knapp, M. L. *Nonverbal Communication In Human Interaction*. New York: Holt, Rinehart and Winston, 1972.

*Lazarus, A. and Fay, A. *I Can If I Want To*. New York: William Morrow, 1975.

Liberman, R. P., King, L. W., DeRisi, W. T. and McCann, M. *Personal Effectiveness: Guiding People to Assert Themselves and Improve their Social Skills*. Champaign: Research Press, 1975.

McDonald, M. "Teaching assertion: A paradigm for therapeutic intervention." *Psychotherapy: Theory, Research and Practice*, 12, 1975, pp. 60–67.

McFall, R. M. and Lillesand, D. B. "Behavior rehearsal with modeling and coaching in assertive training." *Journal of Abnormal Psychology*, 77, 1971, pp. 313–323.

*McMullin, R. E. and Casey, W. W. *Talk Sense To Yourself*. Champaign: Research Press, 1976.

Mehrabian, A. and Wiener, M. "Decoding of inconsistent communication." *Journal of Personality and Social Psychology*, 6, 1967, pp. 108–114.

Meichenbaum, D. "Self-instructional methods." In F. H. Kanfer and A. P. Goldstein, *Helping People Change: A Textbook of Methods*. New York: Pergamon, 1975, pp. 357–392.

Novaco, R. A. "A treatment program for the management of anger through cognitive and relaxation controls." Unpublished doctoral dissertation, Indiana University, Bloomington, Indiana, 1974.

Oakes, W. F. "Reinforcement of Bale's categories in group discussion." *Psychological Reports*, 11, 1962, pp. 427–435.

Obanion, K. "Social anxiety and selective memory for affective information about the self." Unpublished Master's thesis, University of Oregon, 1974.

Osborn, S. A. and Harris, G. *Assertive Training for Women*. Springfield: Charles C. Thomas, 1975.

Paul, G. *Insight vs. Desensitization in Psychotherapy: An Experiment in Anxiety Reduction*. Stanford: Stanford University Press, 1966.

*Phelps, S. and Austin, N. *The Assertive Woman*. San Luis Obispo: Impact, 1975.

Rehm, L. P. and Marston, A. R. "Reduction of social anxiety through modification of self-reinforcement." *Journal of Consulting Psychology*, 32, 1968, pp. 565–574.

Richey, C. A. "Increased female assertiveness through self-reinforcement." Unpublished doctoral dissertation, University of California, Berkeley, 1974.

Rimm, D. C. and Masters, J. C. *Behavior Therapy: Techniques and Empirical Findings*. New York: Academic Press, 1974.

Salter, A. *Conditioned Reflex Therapy*. New York: Farrar, Strauss, 1949.

*Smith, M. J. *When I Say No I Feel Guilty*. New York: Dial Press, 1975.

Suinn, R. M. and Richardson, I. "Anxiety management training: A nonspecific behavior therapy program for anxiety control." *Behavioral Therapy*, 2, 1971, pp. 498–510.

Thorensen, C. E. and Mahoney, M. J. *Behavioral self-control*. New York: Holt, Rinehart and Winston, 1974.

Tighe, T. J. and Elliot, R. "A technique for controlling behavior in natural life settings." *Journal of Applied Behavior Analysis*, 1, 1968, pp. 263–266.

Twentyman, C. T. and McFall, R. M. "Behavioral training of social skills in shy males." *Journal of Consulting and Clinical Psychology*, 43, 1975, pp. 384–395.

Valentine, J. and Arkowitz, H. "Social anxiety and the self-evaluation of interpersonal performance." *Psychological Reports*, 36, 1975, pp. 211–221.

*Watson, D. L. and Tharp, R. G. *Self-directed Behavior: Self Modification for Personal Adjustment*. Monterey: Brooks/Cole, 1972.

Wolpe, J. *The Practice of Behavior Therapy*. Oxford: Pergamon, 1969.

Wolpe, J. and Lazarus, A. *Behavior Therapy Techniques: A Guide to the Treatment of Neurosis*. Oxford: Pergamon, 1966.

Zimbardo, P., Pilkonis, P. A. and Norwood, R. M. "The social disease called shyness." *Psychology Today*, 8, 1975, pp. 69–72.